LETTERS FROM MY FRIEND TEILHARD DE CHARDIN

Teilhard and Pierre Leroy (right) on a Sunday picnic with friends in Peking

LETTERS FROM MY FRIEND TEILHARD DE CHARDIN

1948–1955

Including Letters Written During His Final Years in America

Collected and Introduced by
Pierre Leroy

Translated from the French with a Preface by Mary Lukas

PAULIST PRESS
New York/Ramsey

We wish to thank the following persons for the use of photographs from their collections: Francoise Raphael, George Barbour, Joseph Teilhard de Chardin, Jeanne Mortier, Pierre Leroy, and Malvina Hoffman Properties.

Front cover photograph: R. P. Cordonnier, Saint-Omer

Library of Congress
Catalog Card Number: 80-81883

ISBN: 0-8091-2292-8 (paper)
        0-8091-0310-9 (cloth)

Published by Paulist Press
Editorial Office: 1865 Broadway, New York, N.Y. 10023
Business Office: 545 Island Road, Ramsey, N.J. 07446

Printed and bound in the
United States of America

Preface

When we arrived in France to begin the research for our biography, Teilhard*, the first of his circle of family or acquaintances to offer us his friendship was Father Pierre Leroy. I don't remember who gave us his name or how we found his number, but I do remember that from the moment we phoned him—without knowing anything about us, and in a gesture of instinctive generosity that I would soon learn was part of his personal grace—this closest of Teilhard's confidants suggested we come out at once and visit him. He would have come to us, he said, but he was just recovering from heart surgery and was resting at the Jesuit Ecole Ste. Geneviève near Versailles. Of course, we went. And in the days that followed, he spent hours talking to us both in English and across our still-timorous French, and loading us with documents to take away. Among the first papers we brought back to our hotel were his booklet, Teilhard de Chardin: Tel que je l'ai connu, a red-covered mimeographed copy of Teilhard's then unpublished essay, Le Coeur de la Matière and uncut copies of the present correspondence.

Despite the fact that we had come to France determined to discover the affective and intellectual sources of Teilhard's vision by reading in chronological order all of his works with which we were not familiar and, at the same time, trying to make the acquaintance of his family and friends in the order of their appearance in his life before we really embarked on that enterprise we read these letters Teilhard wrote to Father Leroy. At the time we read them, we did not really realize how

*Mary Lukas and Ellen Lukas, Teilhard. (Garden City: Doubleday & Co. 1977.)

much they were to influence our subsequent understanding of him, or how much the wealth of material we then began to gather was illumined by their light. Not until 1977, in fact, when I read the letters once again, bound in a French edition and very lightly trimmed down by a nervous censor, did I realize how crucial an acquaintance with them is to any understanding of the man Teilhard became, much less to any real comprehension of the meaning and development of his thought.

I was, therefore, delighted to be able to participate in the preparation of this manuscript for an English-speaking audience. Unlike any other collection of his letters thus far published, this book, I can assure the reader, presents Teilhard with face unmasked—and the face it shows is infinitely more attractive than the one his cultist admirers have created. Even more important, these letters present the Teilhardian vision in its most developed form, since they were written during and after the period throughout which he had been in contact with other thinkers of his time, and while he had easy access to scientific journals. This vision is considerably advanced from the one presented in The Phenomenon of Man, (written in China in 1940) with which he remains identified.

Not, of course, that the fundamentals of his worldview ever altered. It was the metaphor in which he expressed it (or perhaps in which it expressed itself to him) that changed as he grew older. Just as the tactile metaphors of stone and iron through which he understood it as a child yielded to the conceptual metaphors of his adult life, so in essay after essay, did he refine the language of these concepts—wrestling like Jacob with the Angel for the words—so that he could communicate these thoughts to others.

As most of the action covered in this correspondence takes place in America, it also seems most appropriate to me that the first English language edition of these letters be presented by an American publisher. To my compatriots, I feel, they give a fascinating picture of "the way we (or our parents) were" in that peculiar little slice of time that was the early Fifties, when the old American dream of the conquest of an endless wilderness had been replaced by the ideal of a Levittown Elysium buzzing with appliances and the cozy chatter of the two-child family, where station wagons stood in the driveways and grey flannel suits hung in closets, when churches were "changeless," monied, proud and sure of their identity, where in a nation which had never lost a war moral and social etiquette were comfortably blocked out and patriotism and anti-patriotism clearly defined, where trust in decent government and faith in the Happy Ending stood unchallenged.

Though no de Toqueville, Teilhard was a man out of an older, wearier culture and one with an eye for social criticism. He could see us, in many ways, more clearly than we could see ourselves; and that bland, innocent country where he came to spend his final years of exile was as much an object of astonishment to him as had been his China-exile of the Thirties and Forties.

In the letters that follow, then, the reader will find a rich potpourri of thought of various kinds. There is gossip about people Teilhard met, political comment, social criticism, and confidences of personal pain and joy such as he gave to no one as freely as he did to Father Leroy. There is also here an almost day-by-day account of Teilhard's projects and ideas—all of it, fortunately (unlike the stiff style of his essays) in the mood of one friend talking to another.

Because of the direction that the search for knowledge took in this epoch these very frank letters of one priest and scientist to another have an unusual excitement. Teilhard had always seen the reconciliation of science and religion as his vocation; and in those last years of Eugenio Pacelli's papal reign, when religion, if anything, was looking backward, science—that science that was born with Galileo and reborn again in the 20th century to such an extent that one can say almost 95% of all we know in science we have learned since 1900—was taking a quantum leap into the future.

In the period immediately following World War II, physics had made enormous strides. The components of the recently split atom were being explored more deeply, and between 1947 and 1954 alone, sixteen new sub-atomic particles were discovered. Biology, too, was moving forward. In 1953 (almost the same month that Teilhard wrote Leroy that "the real weak point of genetics lies in the fact that everything is explained except the genesis of the gene"), Crick and Watson published the paper on the structure of DNA which completely revolutionized genetics.* In anthropology, through the work of southern African scientific teams, and, even more, through the revolutionary work of the Leakeys, Africa took its definitive place as the probable cradle of the human species.

In these letters of Teilhard, which end just before Easter Sunday of 1955, it is bitterly clear that his attempt to readjust the scientific ele-

*Nature, vol. 171 (April 25, 1953), pp. 731–738.

LETTERS FROM MY FRIEND TEILHARD

ments of his vision to the new data so rapidly accumulating was left unfinished. But, since that time, churchmen as well as scientists have begun to realize the importance and validity of the direction in which this vision points. *"The range of impulses [(in Teilhard's work)]," as Cardinal Koenig of Vienna has written recently, "for the whole church and for science, has not even been approximately inventoried."*

In other letters Teilhard wrote before his death to influential ecclesiastical friends, he begged that thinkers take up the task he could not finish. It was his faith that if religion would ally itself with science, it would help to clear away the brush that blocked religion's path to the contemplation of its own truth.

"Not until the church sets out to re-examine the relationship between Christ and a universe now grown fantastically immense and organic," he wrote the bishop of Toulouse in February 1955, would she *"take up her conquering march again."* For pure survival's sake, if nothing else, the Church had no choice but to face up to the task of distinguishing in her theology of the human nature of the Incarnate Word, a 'cosmic' (universe-related) aspect as well as a 'terrestrial' (purely historical) one. And to his immediate superior, André Ravier, Teilhard wrote the same month, *"It seems to me that now, 1500 years later, we are reliving the great struggle of the Arian heresy, with the difference that it is no longer Christ's relationship with the Trinity that is in question, but his relationship to the Universe."**

Large statements all. So large, in fact, that one recoils a bit (as perhaps did Teilhard's bishop friend and his Lyon provincial) at the size of the task to which Teilhard invites us. But by following the development of his ideas in this correspondence, as they daily faced the challenges posed by his unchurched friends, the reader may come more comfortably with him to these conclusions. And by watching their slow growth in his mind through what he lived and learned and over which he agonized, the problem may be brought down to a more comprehensible and manageable size.

Mary Lukas
New York, 1979

---

*The Council of Nicea in 325 A.D. defined Christ's absolute equality with the Father.

viii

Foreword

Teilhard with a young friend in a field in China

Only the most remarkable chain of circumstances could have brought about so long and close a relationship as I was privileged to have with Pierre Teilhard de Chardin. When first we met, I was quite a young scholastic, preparing at the University of Nancy to join the Jesuit missionary explorer Emile Licent at his museum-laboratory at Tientsin, China. Teilhard, on the other hand, a man nineteen years my senior, had already gained considerable recognition from the international scientific community. He had written landmark papers on the fossils of Quercy near Toulouse and on the subdivisions of the Pliocene in the Seine basin; he had traveled the Shensi desert recovering and cataloguing a great deal of material for the Paleontological Museum in Paris; he was already a collaborator in the investigation of the newly discovered Sinanthropus of northern China.

I remember that first short interview in 1928 with utter clarity. Teilhard was passing through Paris on one of his brief home-leaves, and since he knew I was myself en route to China, he agreed to see me. We met in his workroom on the Place Valhubert. I see him still—a tall man in a black suit and a Roman collar, sitting (since he had given me the only chair in the room) casually on the side of his worktable, playing with a piece of chalk. Under his graying hair, his forehead was clear and high,

3

his face deeply etched by sea and desert winds. What struck me most about him at the time was his striking air of something I can only call goodness—a balance of simplicity and courtesy, betraying something of his aristocratic birth—which graced his every move.

I did not expect that interview to be the beginning of a continuing relationship. It was three years before we met again, and then, by purest chance. In the spring of 1931, I was returning on a Chinese junk from a biology field trip along the coastline of the Gulf of Chihli. The pirates who then swarmed the China Sea forced our ship toward land. For three days we lay in Tientsin Harbor before docking. When we docked at last, I set out at once for the Jesuit school there and for Licent's museum. For some reason I remember it was a Sunday.

As I started up toward Race Course Road, I saw a figure coming toward me. It was, to my surprise, Teilhard. I had expected that at that moment he would be serving with the eastern arm of the Citroën company's Yellow Expedition* in the Gobi. But here he was in Tientsin. I was delighted to find him just as I remembered him: black clerical suit and Roman collar (this time with a light overcoat), head down a little to the right, arms outstretched in welcome. And again, half-hidden under the brim of his black hat, that unforgettable smile.

In the years that followed, Teilhard, who was then attached to the Chinese Geological Survey in Peking, came from time to time to visit the school of Hautes Etudes on Race Course Road. But it was not until the world exploded into a second great World War, and he and I, and one Father Minister who managed the house, were shut up together for five years of semi-isolation in the ancient Chinese capital, that our relationship took root. Throughout those years of separation from the world at home, of relative deprivation and of an intimately shared scien-

---

*In early 1931, the Citroën automobile company, under the direction of Georges-Marie Haardt, undertook a motor crossing through Asia from Beirut to Peking. The Chinese arm of the expedition in which Teilhard had agreed to take part was scheduled to head west from Kalgan in April of that year, but was delayed by a mechanical breakdown. M.L.

tific, social and religious life, this relationship grew and deepened. The difference in our ages never seemed an obstacle. During that time, I never felt anything but completely at ease in the company of that great thinker, so generous, so modest, and—despite the dismal situation in which we found ourselves—so full of warmth and humor.

With a second explosion—that of the bomb at Hiroshima—the war came to an end. Our isolation ended, leaving us with but a single thought: to return to Paris, liberated the year before, and to renew the contacts from which the war had separated us. We knew we were returning to a world in ruins, and we had no precise idea of how we would serve in it. But we knew we must go back. After waiting conscientiously for all the clerical permissions that he needed to return, Teilhard left Peking in March 1946 and arrived in May 1946 at the residence of the writers of Etudes. After a series of bizarre accidents which drew the short plane trip I had counted on into a two-month odyssey, I, too, arrived in France.

Over the next two years in Paris, Teilhard and I met often. But after 1948, his and my various short trips, my year-long stay in Chicago, and finally his final exile to America at just about the moment I was going back to France, made our separation permanent. Through the period, it was by letter that we kept in touch. And it was through these letters that I was able to follow the development of the life and thought of my friend until his death.

At the urging of those who know how close Teilhard and I were in his later years, and after considerable hesitation, I have decided to publish these letters which I so carefully preserved. Their familiar tone and their relative absence of technical jargon sets them apart, in form more than in content, from all Teilhard has written in his books and essays. It was not as a teacher that he spoke to me, but as a friend. Hence the telegraphic economy of the allusions, the impulsive flashes of irony and humor, and the quick spur-of-the-moment protests that were his immediate reaction to individual events in the progressive destruction of all he held most dear—reactions which (even at the moment they were uttered) do not betray the slightest meanspiritedness or spite, and which always settled down under the influence of time and reflection, as Teilhard resigned himself to his fate.

Anyone who searches these letters for a closed system of philosophic thought will seek in vain. Here it is Teilhard the man who speaks. It is he who observes, reacts and judges. It is he who records the events of daily life—he who discusses projects in hand, he who notes his disappointments and his joys, he who describes his nostalgia for the sky of China and his astonishment before new landscapes.

But just as sharply present here as is the unmasked face of the man I knew so well and so admired, is the unquestionable evidence of the two passions that drove him: his unfaltering devotion to the living Christ, and his unswerving fidelity to a pre-Vatican II church, which he so desperately hoped would open itself more freely to the needs of modern man. Reinforced by the urgency of the human voice beneath it, it is, above all, Teilhard's preoccupation with these two great loves that speaks from this collection.

In releasing these letters for publication, it is, of course, my hope that they will give some pleasure to the readers of Teilhard who wish to know him better. But even more, it is my prayer that they may help to clarify and reinforce for them the message to which he devoted his long life: his conviction that the evolutionary movement which presses us forward (En Avant), just as surely drives us upward (En Haut); and his certainty that the slow, progressive rise of consciousness in evolution can only be truly understood in terms of a reach for union with the Divine.

May this little book bring to all who take it up—whether they seek it in the heart of their own historic adventure or in the bosom of a Church condemned to suffering and contradiction— the Light and Strength that science alone is powerless to supply.

Pierre Leroy

1946-1947

Teilhard at Les Moulins in Auvergne

**W**ith the end of World War II, after seven years of exile and shared confinement during the Japanese occupation of Peking—a period whose monotony was as difficult to bear as its material privation—Teilhard and I suddenly found ourselves free to return to France. While I, clinging to the hope of going back to China one day, waited for a flight to bring me quickly and directly home, Teilhard, who wanted to bring back to France his heavy baggage with all his notes, essays and publications, decided to go by boat.

RETURN TO FRANCE

We parted on the Peking airstrip on March 15, 1946. The commandant of the American First Marine Division in Northeast China, Gen. William A. Worton, had put a plane at Teilhard's disposal to help him make the hop to Shanghai where he could find a ship. As we waited on the tarmac, I remember that the cold was piercing and that ice coated the wings of the plane as it took off into a graying sky. On his arrival at the port, my friend was lucky enough to secure a berth on an English steamer, the Strathmore, which had been outfitted for the repatriation of Europeans. He left China within the week.

9

LETTERS FROM MY FRIEND TEILHARD

After a long sea voyage, he arrived in Paris on May 3. The same day he moved back into his old room in the house at 15 Rue Monsieur where the staff of Etudes *was quartered. There he found the circle of old friends and brothers in religion who had always been a sure support for him.*

It was, however, in a climate of uncertainty and stress that Teilhard, already worn down by the long fatigue of the Japanese occupation and weakened by lack of medical care and poor nourishment, took up his work. From the beginning, his health was very fragile.

He had already suffered nervous crises in 1939 and again in 1940. In the following years, new crises, less violent and equally ill-defined, repeated themselves, without anyone's attaching much importance to them.

SICKNESS AND CONVALESCENCE

Once back in France, however, the tension under which Teilhard was working built to climax. The night of May 31–June 1, he was stricken with a serious heart attack. The other Fathers of the house had him transported immediately to the Hospital of the Brothers of St. John of God on the nearby Rue Oudinot. During his confinement there, his physical discomfort was somewhat eased by two small consolations: he was elected corresponding member of the Academy of Sciences; and he was promoted to the grade of officer in the Legion of Honor.

On June 25, he left the hospital and began a period of convalescence at the rest home of the Sisters of the Immaculate Conception at Saint-Germain-en-Laye.

He knew that the attack had been a bad one. When I visited him, both at the Rue Oudinot and then at Saint-Germain, he made no attempt to hide his pain. Would he still be able to continue his anthropological studies? Wouldn't the restrictions now imposed on him by his illness force him to forego work in the field? It was several years now since he had sent The Phenomenon of Man—*the manuscript that he felt represented so much of his life's work—to Rome. But no permission ever came to publish it.*

By October 2, 1947, Teilhard was back at the Rue Monsieur, ostensibly to stay. He had yielded up to four months of prescribed rest—four months of restrictions of the kind with which he was totally incapable of reconciling his vocation. He made no secret of how much this state of forced inactivity was costing him. But his spirit seemed to draw strength from the weakness of his body. As soon as he was able, he went back to work. He prepared and delivered lectures, and spent a great part of his time receiving an ever-growing number of friends. More than ever, he sought out people who, though they did not share his religious ideas, were in agreement with his faith in human destiny. He took open pleasure in the company of these eager and exacting minds which were often ready to receive his message.

Still, his growing influence in Paris disturbed the religious authorities. They made it clear that his presence in France was unwelcome. Thus, despite the support of many of his scientific and religious colleagues, he continued to feel ill at ease. As further restrictions were laid on his activities, his discomfort grew. Happily, soon after his return from Saint-Germain, an opportunity to leave Paris arose. He was invited to visit New York. He eagerly accepted, made a reservation on the America, and sailed on February 25. (1 9 4 8)

Apart from one stormy day at sea, the voyage was without incident. In New York, two old friends were waiting on the dock.

1948-1950

St. Peter's Square, Rome

A t first, post-war America struck Teilhard like a breath of fresh air. He was staying with the Jesuit Fathers of the magazine America where John LaFarge, "a friend of many years;" William C. Nevils, the intelligent and unusually open superior of the house; and Robert Graham, whom he had met at a Jesuit symposium in Versailles in August 1947, all received him warmly.

AMERICA

Just the same, it did not take Teilhard very long to measure the distance that separated him from his American Jesuit brethren and from American Catholics in general. Their understanding and practice of the Faith had little in common with his aspirations for it. The sectarianism of the American church, its rivalry with Protestantism, and its tendency to draw apart from the mainstream of American life bewildered him. Nor could he come to terms with the predilection of American priests for building churches, schools and universities, and, in general, for managing money as though they were only businessmen.

The political climate of the place aggravated his discomfort. In Europe, the church stood embattled before the communist threat in the Italian elections; in America, the anticommunist

LETTERS FROM MY FRIEND TEILHARD

McCarthyite hysteria was at its height. Teilhard understood the "witch-hunt" as a phenomenon which "confounded evil with change . . ." The misunderstanding disturbed him deeply and gave political overtones to much of what he wrote.

During the visit, Teilhard stopped by the American Museum of Natural History, where he had had many friends. The connection was not so fruitful as he had hoped. Though he joyfully rediscovered his old colleague the paleontologist, Walter Chaney, (celebrated for his discovery in China of the fossilized remains of the ancestor of the modern sequoia tree) and a little later the Swiss parasitologist, Reinhold Hoppeli, whom he had known at the Peking Union Medical College in China, and whose caustic humor amused him, there were other friends he missed—the paleontologist, Walter Granger, who had died shortly before, and Ralph von Koenigswald, the discoverer of the Pithecanthropus of Java who had gone home to Europe to teach. The only other member of the staff he knew was Franz Weiderreich, a solemn and serious paleontologist with whom he had worked on the Peking Man in China and who now was permanently attached to the Museum.

In the weeks that followed, Teilhard sought out other American acquaintances from China who lived in New York and Washington. He took the opportunity of seeing his old friend, Childs Frick, a kind of modern Maecenas, who had put together an extraordinary collection of fossil mammals, and whose passionate interest in human origins Teilhard admired. Curiously enough, it was about this time that Teilhard said of his own once-burning passion for the past, "I am now experiencing a kind of nausea for fossils. Explain that to me, if you can . . ." Oriented as he then definitively was toward the study of man, he wished to multiply his contacts with like-minded people and to explore the possibilities for man's future. But the question remained: what means would he take to do it?

Since the opportunity arose for him to give a series of six conferences at American universities the following year, he hoped to follow up the project. He applied to the Jesuit American Provincial for approval; before giving it, the superior re-

ferred the matter on to Rome. There the project rested. Aside from one lecture at the Wenner-Gren, Teilhard gave no important public conferences during this visit to America.

Though frequently misrepresented and misunderstood, he continued to talk to individual people and to write. He felt quite strongly that even those Christians who worked in fields connected with what he called "the Science of Man" did not really understand the potentialities of their calling. To be effective, it seemed to him there were two premises they would have to realize a priori. *These were a faith in the promise of technology, properly utilized (the forward progress, or progress* En Avant*), and a faith in humanity's final self-surpassing destiny (the upward progress, or progress* En Haut*). These two ideas are summed up in the Teilhardian expression "ultra-anthropogenesis."*

Since he was always forced to coin new words to express his thought, Teilhard has not always been understood by his readers. Abstract expressions can often be misleading. By "ultra-anthropogenesis," Teilhard meant the progressive rise of the human biologic group toward a final Goal, which Man, left to himself and considered apart from God, is not even capable of imagining. As he saw it, the development of a more and more complex human society is an organic process, and, as such, follows general laws of biology. To the easily observable fact that mankind moves forward toward the future, must, Teilhard believed, be added the faith-deduced fact that a "spiritual" attraction, pulling from above is exercised by Christ over the whole of creation—and especially over man.

It is for this reason that in Teilhard's thought the vision of evolution remains incomplete unless it is linked with a Christology. Naturally, there can be no question of deducing from "cosmogenesis" such revealed truths as the unfathomable mystery of the Incarnation. Teilhard's "ultra-anthropogenesis," then, must fundamentally be seen as an attempt to recognize the harmony between the idea of man as explained by biology, and man as understood by Christian doctrine. In other words, where man is most himself, there God must be.

LETTERS FROM MY FRIEND TEILHARD

During the months when Teilhard visited America in 1948, he enclosed, in one letter to me, a short note which explained Life in the universe as "the activity of the cosmos"—a murky hypothesis, to be sure, if taken by itself. He very quickly, however, clarified his meaning. "The heart of my vision," he wrote in a subsequent letter, "is to try to see in living particles tangible centers of emergence for the whole of the cosmic force."

Later, he made his point even more sharply by explaining that, rather than being just an "accidental, localized anomaly," each living thing in the cosmos constitutes a "point of incandescence" in that otherwise opaque phenomenon which is Creation.

Given what we now know of molecular biology, Teilhard's intuition of thirty years ago shows him to us, even then, directly on the track of the probable solution to the question of the emergence of life. Who does not now agree that the chemicals for the building of the macro-molecules which are the basis of life are drawn from the universe as a whole? Other factors are, of course, required for the organization of such molecules; Teilhard never denied this. He simply evoked the theoretically valid generalization that the same physico-chemical processes are at work, not only in our solar system, but in other galaxies as well. It was, for its time, an adventurous assumption.

March 1, 1948

AMERICA
National Catholic Weekly
329 West 108th St.
New York, 25, N.Y.

My Dear Friend,

Well, here I am at last in America—just a bit surprised (but agreeably so) at having cast my moorings off and at breathing freely—a most rejuvenating feeling. But where is all this leading?—Still difficult to say.

18

The sea voyage was without incident. We left at night from Cherbourg in a soft flurry of snow. Stopped a few hours in the fog just south of Ireland (Cobh). The weather was cold but bracing, except for one really stormy day when some dishes were broken and other articles (including my berth, which slid with me on it, all the way across the cabin) were bounced about. Of course, we had first-class comfort and great speed (600 miles a day). But a five-day trip is too short to make many new acquaintances among the other passengers, unless one already knows someone aboard. My one interesting contact was with a Parisian businessman, a bit on the conservative side, but receptive. He just happened to have with him the issue of the weekly magazine in which the critic with the pseudonym V. was critical of me.

At the dock, I found R. and L. waiting for me . . .

. . . My first contacts with the American Museum of Natural History and with the Jesuits here went off well. Here at America House, besides Father LaFarge, a friend of many years, and the superior, Father Nevils, very open, though along in years), I've seen a good deal of young Father Graham, an observer at the U.N. whom I first met at the "jamboree" at Versailles last August. My welcome to the house was cordial and gruff, as is the custom here. To tell the truth, though, I still do not really feel spiritually at ease in this setting. I have the impression that for both the American priests and laity, Christianity means hiding the world, rather than revealing it—but maybe I'm prejudiced. With a little more experience, I may change my mind. Well, perhaps . . .

At the American Museum, I was enthusiastically received. Granger's death, however, leaves a great void. I missed von Koenigswald by a few days; he had left to teach at Utrecht. Weidenreich has not changed much. He's still very active and about to publish a remarkable treatise on *Homo Soloensis.* I still haven't seen Frick. Did I tell you that in rediscovering this paleontological milieu I've felt with considerable sharpness (a sharpness I admit I expected) that except in those things which concern human origins (and curiously enough, in things which concern the formation of the continents—perhaps because this touches a "planetary" problem), I now feel a certain nausea for the study of the Past? This feeling certainly does not throw light on my immediate future. I ask myself, technically speaking, what am I going to do here in the next few weeks? Doubtless, very little. On the other hand, I very much want to multiply my contacts with new people. I vaguely sense (or better still, I have a presentiment) that Providence perhaps has put me here for some very definite purpose still unclear to me. And so I wait. I'm still a long way from having taken a good look at the situation around me, even in New York alone.

Judging from the newspapers, political storm-clouds are gathering in Europe. I'm afraid of being taken in by propaganda. But there are some ominous signs, just the same. Wouldn't it be absurd if I were again absent from Europe when something catastrophic happened? You know what I'm thinking. If it is to respond adequately to the movement which is forcing it to tighten on itself, the world will have to remake itself on the psychological level. From this point of view, who's to say that, even in the interest of the kingdom of God, a good dip into Marxism right now may not be the very thing we need to save us?

"Quis ascendit nisi qui descendit."
More later. Meanwhile, best to all,

TEILHARD

March 20, 1948

AMERICA
National Catholic Weekly
329 West 108th St.
New York 25, N.Y.

Dear Friend,

Thanks for your letter of the 15th which arrived yesterday
. . . As far as the meetings at Lejay's* are concerned, I feel just as
you do. But don't be afraid of snuffing out a struggling flame.
There is something really useful going on in his discussions,
though only in a first approximation. The problem lies in the atmosphere that surrounds Lejay's gatherings. Whereas you and I
and many others can no longer conceive of a religion that does
not magnify and intensify our vision of creation, too many of
Lejay's people, because of *a priori* reservations, wear their Christianity like a pair of blinkers to shut out the grandeur and the
value of the world.—To tell the truth, I really think that this is
what lies at the heart of the spiritual problem of the modern
world. Nothing (Christianity included) can possibly hold together (much less grow) unless it has faith in an earthly human
process directed upwards.

Here in New York, I follow the same uncertain existence,
with no precise work to do, still undecided about my future,
even though I go on seeing many different kinds of people. I
still have a vague sense that but for (or perhaps thanks to) this
agitation, I continue to be drawn in the direction of that still
nameless science which will give us the biological outline for the
general conditions of "ultra-anthropogenesis."

I did tell you, didn't I, that I'm going to give my lecture in
the upstairs library of the Viking Fund. This evening at Weidenreich's I ran into Hoppeli again . . .

Affectionately,
TEILHARD

*Pierre Lejay. Jesuit geo-physicist whose Thursday afternoon salons attracted
the cream of Christian priest-scientists in Paris.(ML)

LETTERS FROM MY FRIEND TEILHARD

April 15, 1948

AMERICA
National Catholic Weekly
329 West 108th Street
New York 25, N.Y.

Dear Friend,

Thanks so much for your Easter letter. . . .
. . . I've just come back from Washington, where spring was at its loveliest. The woods of Virginia were still dark with winter but gleaming with transparent greens, pinks and scarlet. I saw many of our old China friends, notably Maria Wilhelm, the Grews, the Lyonses (their daughter whom I baptized in China is a young lady now) and others. Lucile Swan and Eleanor Tafel live there five minutes from Georgetown University. If you had been there with me there we could have had a real family reunion!

In Washington I established (or rather, reestablished) two good contacts with Catholic University: Father Connolly, a quite receptive specialist in the study of the brain; and Father Cooper, an ethnologist. They welcomed me most warmly. Still, I'm afraid people there are not very adventurous.

I have, however, managed to give two little talks in one month. Yesterday I spoke at the American Museum on the geological genesis of Eastern Asia, and last Friday at the Viking Fund on "Direction and Significance of Human Evolution" to a group of anthropologists. I was quite surprised at how easily— even passionately—I was able to express myself in English. I think it went off well. Sometime in May, I'll probably do the same thing at Harvard. Then, next year, I hope to give a series of six conferences at Columbia or Harvard—provided the authorities don't stop me. With all this going on, I'm thinking of holding off on returning to France until the end of June. Quite a few good contacts are turning up among the Jesuits here. Last Sunday, for instance, four Nathaniels came to see me one evening and I spoke to them two hours at a stretch, in a very ortho-

22

dox way I hope, about important subjects. All that I said to you before about my first impression of the clergy here remains the same. But decidedly there is more to hope for than I thought. Many young and semi-young people need only reverse the lens through which they observe reality . . . .

Fraternally yours in Christ,
TEILHARD

P.S.

Let me know whether or not my article has appeared in the *Revue des Questions Scientifiques* of April 15*. It seems to me that St. Seine hasn't received my proofs. Do give him my best regards. And thank him for his letter.

I approve of the Pope's attitude [re communism] as good strategic play. But I'm afraid that under the political gesture, I sense dogmatic overtones. Dangerous, that! And one more example of the confusion between evil and change.

Here we're all waiting for Jouve to arrive tomorrow!

Had a long visit with Georges Le Fèvre, now returning from Texas and Venezuela. Civilization (or spiritualization) by means of petrol! We must talk about this subject later—Just saw George Barbour in Washington and here.

Affectionately,
TEILHARD

---

*"The Rebound of Human Evolution and Its Consequences," *Revue des Questions Scientifiques*, April 20, 1948.

LETTERS FROM MY FRIEND TEILHARD

April 24,1948

AMERICA
National Catholic Weekly
329 West 108th St.
New York 25, N.Y.

Dear Friend,

Thank you for your letter of the 14th which must have crossed mine in the mail. . . . Like it or not, there is a certain fatality in the relentlessness with which research organizes itself, just as society does, and for the same reasons. It is disappointing to realize how often in this area (as in that of the faith in the future that the effort of discovery implies) so many good researchers are still children—or even schoolboys—incapable of analyzing or criticizing their action. To make this point, I'm enclosing a clip from yesterday's *New York Times* that shows how undervalued is the work of a research team in this country.

Here I find the possibilities for work quite interesting since, if the Order doesn't interfere, I have an offer to give a series of six conferences (on "The Place and Structure of Humanity") next spring in just the kind of university I would have chosen. I am going to start to take some prudent steps vis-à-vis the Company that I'll tell you about later.

Otherwise things are pretty much the same. There's general rejoicing in the house over the arrival of Jouve, who has proceeded to charm everyone. Yesterday I saw my dear friend Chaney from Berkeley. He has just come back from the Szechuan basin southeast of Chunking where he went to study the remains of some Tertiary forests which contained, besides a group of known species, a kind of conifer related to the sequoia—a species that we thought had disappeared. The trip was only a month long, but it was difficult. And Chaney brought back a painful impression of China.

Towards the 10th of May, I plan to go to Boston. I still haven't been able to make a reservation on a boat going home in June, but I'm told if I'm patient, something will turn up. People

24

here have calmed down after the Italian elections, but it seems to me like the relief that follows terror—all of which does not prove anything about the present human vitality of the Christian faith!

Affectionately,
TEILHARD

May 23, 1948

AMERICA
National Catholic Weekly
329 West 108th Street
New York 25, N.Y.

Very Dear Friend,

Thank you for your letter of the 19th and for all the news it brought me. I'm glad to hear your projects for next year are clearing up. As far as my own problems go—my plans for the six conferences for Columbia or elsewhere, scheduled for the spring of 1949, are still up in the air (or did I already tell you?) since the Provincial here is determined to refer the matter to Rome. I have already alerted d'Ouince. And as I can't see that I really have anything more of importance to do here right now, I will be coming home on June 5 on a fast Dutch ship (the *New Amsterdam*) which stops at Le Havre—I really should be satisfied. But at this moment I am undergoing one of those periods of nervous depression such as you witnessed two or three times in Peking. Everything seems mountainous to me. Patience! I hope that my distress will pay or serve for something.—In any case, I'm leaving here. I don't feel I'm achieving anything. Nothing is going on; everyone is on vacation. I visited Boston (Harvard) last week but saw very few people besides the anthropologists (Movius, Houghton). I did, however, meet one physiologist, a Northern Irelander named Crozier who wrote "The Physiology of Vision" and who knows Tessier, Grassé, etc. I found him very sympathetic and chatted with him about "The Great Questions." And *apropos* "the Questions," I think your problem (and the subject of the note I sent you with my last letter) is that you still look on life as a kind of interruption in the evolutionary process—something not entirely integral to it. The heart of my vision, on the other hand, lies in understanding living particles (and *a fortiori*, "grains of thought") as the real centers of emergence for the whole of the "Cosmic Pressure." Man can, in fact, be placed at the intersection of two processes: molecularization (which concerns the cell) and siderealization (the process of the formation of the stars, which includes the cellular systems at the surface of the earth). Think about it. In this redirection of thinking, wherein every living particle becomes a point of "incandescence" of the universe rather than a local and accidental anomaly, I see an essential element of the foundation for any rational and Christian *Weltanschauung.*—There is, of course, no question of displacing the idea of "Finality." The concept of a Universe which centers organically and which includes, as a co-relative, the development of consciousness is just as legitimate as—and more complete than—the concept of "a universe which expands."

With best wishes to d'Ouince, etc.

Most affectionately in Xt,
TEILHARD

RETURN TO PARIS

The four-month visit to America did not end satisfactorily. Frustrated in his projects and ill at ease in his intellectual solitude, Teilhard came back to Paris earlier than he had planned.

He left on June 5 for Le Havre on a Dutch ship. When he arrived at the Gare Saint-Lazare in the afternoon, I was waiting for him. I had expected to find the same old friend of happier days. But instead, I saw, climbing down from the train, a broken man who threw himself into my arms and burst into tears, powerless to put two syllables together. It took a great deal of effort on my part to find out what the problem was. And when I did, it turned out to be practically nothing. After stopping at customs at Le Havre, Teilhard had simply forgotten to lock the case that contained his papers and he was in terror of having lost them.

I accompanied him back to Etudes. *But when the dinner hour came, he refused to leave his room. He begged me not to leave him, and I tried, without success, to comfort him. Finally I remembered one of the remarks he himself had made to others when they were in great pain. Placing his crucifix before him, I reminded him that the cross was not empty, but that the image of the God-Man was there. He returned me so sorrowful a look that I automatically took him into my arms, if only to give him a little human warmth.*

Eventually though, his daily life took up its measured pace once more. Again, telephone conversations, private meetings and visits began to absorb his day. Toward the middle of August, very fatigued, he left for Moulins near Clermont-Ferrand in Auvergne, to stay at the house of his brother, Joseph, who himself was then suffering deeply over the recent accidental death of his son. Teilhard went home to rest; but worry followed him. He, who so much wished to taste the blessed peace of the Divine Presence, was in complete interior conflict. It was the kind of discouragement which would easily have defeated another man and robbed him of all hope. But not Teilhard. He drove himself onward beyond personal difficulties and continued to work toward making the reality of his Point Omega more accessible to himself and others.

In order to reach that Point, nonetheless, he had to pass through the crucible of suffering and personal purification through which all the friends of God must go.

The lessons of abandonment which Teilhard's letters written before the end of 1948 have to give us are extremely precious. In them we will see him accepting the probable loss of the one thing which was closest to his heart: his life's work, The Phenomenon of Man." *The manuscript could not receive the approval of the religious censors who were still so ill prepared to understand it. Its publication would be put off sine die; and it would be in the city of Rome itself that Teilhard would have his first real intuition of that eventuality. There, at the heart of Christianity, he would measure the bitter consequences of the "prudence" of those who were unable to follow the thought of a pioneer so in advance of his times.*

Les Moulins, August 28, 1948

Dear Friend,

Thank you for your very welcome letter of the 25th, which arrived yesterday. It reached me in the extraordinary peaceful setting of Moulins, and in soft, sweet weather. As I write you, I can see from my window first a flock of wooded hills (we are at an altitude of about 400 meters), then the end of the Limagne, then, forming the skyline, the whole chain of volcanoes from Mount Dore to the puys. Puy-de-Dôme is just before me to the west. It really should be quite relaxing here. But still, I remain fairly (on the physical plain I could say *viscerally*) anxious. As I told you, it's a recurrence, perhaps even worse, of my nervous attacks of 1939. In one sense, I wonder if the relative absence of action and distraction does not make me feel it all the more.— Fundamentally, I believe that the less I think about my problems, the better. But this distress certainly does not give me much strength for the various obligations of the next few months—especially for the trip to Rome. Next week, I will probably try to make a kind of retreat to put myself back in the Presence and in the Heart of God.

Since my arrival (nearly fifteen days ago) I've written several letters, some supplementary notes to "Comment je crois," which is presently being retyped and reduplicated by a friend, and I've at last written out ten or so pages to accompany the corrected bibliography for my possible eventual candidacy at the Collège de France. At times I walk about here with my brother, who shows me his farms. My other two sisters-in-law come calling on us. These visits, and the permanent presence of the new du Passage ménage (a great success!) brighten the old house which has such a need of gaiety. The memory of my nephew, who was, as you know, drowned in this very place last year, fills everything like a shadow simultaneously gentle and sad—like the presence (as I said to friends) of someone who one feels has "just stepped from a room" at the moment that one enters it. My brother's serenity is admirable. . . .

. . . Thank you for the news you sent me. I'm still thinking of coming back on September 15, but in what kind of political atmosphere? Will we have de Gaulle or Thorez?

Meanwhile, my deep affection,
TEILHARD

P.S.

There is surely something that should be further pursued in your idea of the spiritual frustration of modern Christians. At the present time, no religion explicitly and officially offers us the God we need. This is why it seems to me so fundamental that we rethink our Christology, in order to show "the Christ Universal" to the world.

ROME

The first project on Teilhard's calendar after his return to Paris was his preparation for the Roman visit. The trip had been arranged a bit precipitously. With the retirement of his friend, the Abbé Breuil, there was a vacant place at the Collège de France; and in the beginning of November, after careful preparation on Breuil's part, Teilhard was to present his candidacy for the post. Before doing so, however, he had to obtain the authorization of the General of his Order. Time was very short. Teilhard arrived in Rome at midnight October 4–5, 1948.

Contrary to his expectations, he was welcomed at the Curia with a warmth that quite overwhelmed him. "I was extremely graciously received," he wrote. The phrase says much. The Fa-

thers of the house showed him great affection and immediately made him feel "part of the family." For, if his reputation as an innovator was well established with the Romans, so also was their awareness of the regularity of his religious life and his obedience. The correspondence which follows on these pages will show how firm this obedience stood, under the strongest pressures.

In his reflections on the city of Rome, Teilhard wrote that even though he felt at ease in the southern light and brilliant colors, the city itself woke little enthusiasm in him. Much more significant is his reaction to the sight of St. Peter's basilica which, despite its baroque vastness and the symbolic switches that stood by its confession boxes, moved him, since he saw in it a kind of physical planetary center of Christianity.

After St. Peter's it was the mother church of the Jesuits which touched him most. In the seventeenth century, the Fathers had constructed a great church they called the Gesù, a new architectural conception which came to be much imitated. In order that preachers should be better understood, the church, built in the form of a cross, had only a single nave; and at the end of each of its two arms stood chapels, in this case, one altar dedicated to St. Ignatius Loyola (the founder of the Order) and one to the Madonna della Strada. St. Ignatius always had a particular devotion to this Virgin of pilgrims, and just before leaving for the missions, most of the Jesuits of Rome came here to pray. Such "family souvenirs" had meaning for Teilhard. But since he feared that his emotion might be incorrectly interpreted, he wryly added in his letter to me the warning, "Don't get the idea that I've become so sentimental that I'm going soft at last."

In Teilhard's Roman letters, the major idea of his personal vocation is expressed with clarity and force: "Mankind," he wrote, "is in the process of crossing a real threshold, and people in high places here imagine it's just a passing phase." The letters written from this place give one a better appreciation of the ideas that Teilhard defended throughout the course of his life, *and for which he was ready to submit to an interior martyrdom. The slow wear and tear of one rebuff after another would have broken a lesser man. How many indeed in our time have abandoned youthful vocations and broken promises, however solemn, in order to affirm the rights they discovered in maturity. Teilhard, however, was a man of another stamp. He knew what he owed to the Order, and had no illusions what would happen to his mission if he were to break with it definitively. And if he chose to be a secular priest, would things really have been easier for him? The censure against such ideas as he held was the same for everyone. Or, if he chose instead to be reduced to the lay state, what would the profit be? Not only would he betray the calling he so deeply cherished, he would, at the same time, thoroughly discredit both himself and his ideas in the Church's eyes.*

While Teilhard was in Rome, the Jesuit Curia (the name given to the building where the administrative services of the Order were assembled, and where the Father General, his assistants, and the heads of various bureaus live) revived other memories. In Peking, a Canadian Jesuit named Marin had founded a Jesuit house of studies dedicated to Noël Chabanel, a French missionary murdered in the 17th century by the Iroquois. It was there that young Jesuits newly come from Europe, Canada and the Americas used to pass an obligatory two years in studying Chinese. Chabanel House was ruled in a severe and austere fashion; and when Teilhard was in Peking, before the foundation of our Institute of Geobiology, he stayed there. Chinese in conception, his little cell was tiny, and its furniture very worn. But this disturbed him little. Much more of a difficulty for him was the spirit which prevailed in the house. The demands of the Father Superior made the atmosphere more strict than that of a novitiate; the minutiae of a Rule, conceived as if it were addressed to very young people, created an artificial world, quite unlike the one most of the Fathers had known in their native countries. Like many others, Teilhard fitted in there rather badly, and bore the inevitable out of sheer virtue. In Rome, though the atmosphere of the Curia was somewhat less strict, Teilhard, nevertheless, felt he breathed the air of Chabanel again.

31

LETTERS FROM MY FRIEND TEILHARD

In the Jesuit curia, however, many Fathers just returned from China were reunited, bringing with them much news not readily available in Paris. Teilhard learned, for instance, that René Charvet, the superior of the mission under whose jurisdiction he had lived his last years in Asia, and who had been imprisoned by the Communists, was finally liberated.

After many days of waiting, my friend did at last have his long-sought interview with the Father General. Though the exchange seemed to go well, he was given no immediate answer to his problems. Teilhard quickly learned that a decision would not come easily. In Rome, his patience was being tested once again. And waiting aside, how was he to occupy himself?

Teilhard's letter of October 30 contains nothing new, except the announcement of his return to Paris. Things continued to move slowly; he still had no answers to the important questions for which he had made his trip. After the arrival of a first criticism, his book did not receive the approval of the censors. A second criticism arrived, and he still received no nihil obstat.

We have spoken about Teilhard's "anxious" temperament, but even though he had one, he still often managed to be "philosophic" about his fate. In Rome, he was "amused" to see how much the very word "Evolution" seemed to frighten everybody. In his free time, he visited various quarters of the city, and one night met the fiercest of his critics, Reginald Garrigou-Lagrange, a powerful Dominican who had not the slightest understanding of his philosophical and theological effort and who had always used his influence against him. When, at last, they faced one another, one might have expected a heated argument—or at least discussion. But no. "We smiled," Teilhard wrote me, "and talked about Auvergne." People from Peking—Gabriel Beauroy from the French Embassy and Diane de Margerie whom Teilhard had seen grow up in the Chinese capital—were among other old friends whom Teilhard rejoiced to meet again in Rome. Also, there was his old acquaintance, René Arnou, one-time director of the literary studies which young Jesuits then had to make after their novitiate. Called to Rome toward 1925, Arnou had taught philosophy, then theology, and finally became Dean of the Gregorian University.

After his liberation from China, René Charvet had come to Rome to discuss with Jean-Baptiste Janssens, the Father-General, the missionaries' situation in a China that gave every evidence of wanting no more of them. Teilhard was at the Curia at the moment when Charvet arrived. The old superior had a great admiration for Teilhard, and one may easily imagine the tone of their conversation after two years of separation.

And then at the end of that letter are these words: "Tomorrow, the feast of Christ the King. Oh, Rue Labrousse!" It was a reference to the Institute of Geobiology on the Rue Labrousse in Peking where Teilhard and I had lived during the war. By common agreement, we made the feast of Christ the King our patronal day. In 1948, the feast was celebrated on October 31, the last Sunday of the month.

Borgo S. Spirito 5, Roma, October 15, 1948

Very Dear Friend,

I've been here over a week, living in these sacred precincts where I never thought I'd be, and where, incidentally, I was most graciously received. It is, therefore, time to send you news and some impressions. I have already outlined the most important of these in a letter to Father d'Ouince, who may perhaps already have repeated them to you. First of all, I should tell you that Rome neither gave me, nor I expect, will give me, any aesthetic or spiritual shock. It was as I expected. As far as the Past is concerned, I am immune to it; and as far as picturesqueness goes, after Asia, nothing can surprise me. On the other hand, I immediately felt at ease in this southern and colorful setting. And more important, I began to sense (at St. Peter's only) how true it is that Christianity is a phenomenon unto itself ("The Christian Phenomenon," I was right!) with its paradoxical, but incontrovertibly efficacious, consciousness of being the earthly tip of the arch rising from Man to That which is beyond him. Before this great fact (as I told d'Ouince) the swelling baroque of the churches, the symbolic penitent's switches of the confessionals, and the most frightful display of ecclesiastical accoutrements one can conceive of, fade into nothingness. It is this and nothing else that makes going to Rome worth while.

After St. Peter's and only a little less so, it was the church of the Gesù which, up to now, touched me most deeply.—Yes, the Gesù—despite its swarming statues, its moldings, and its extraordinary paintings and frescoes (here a wing, there a leg, as one would say in a cartoon) which hang down over the cornices and columns. I admit to having been much moved at the altar of St. Ignatius and even more so in the little chapel of the Madonna della Strada. So many great men prayed before that image—family souvenirs, memories of a religious childhood, and then, above all in that place, the awareness of how really great the Order is.—Please don't get the idea I've become so sentimental that I'm going soft. What I think that I am feeling is that here, in the Roman climate, both my attachments and my distaste affirm and clarify themselves with equal force.

The vital necessity that Christianity faced with the contemporary neo-humanism (evolutionary and biological) should recognize it, feel it, take hold of it and Christify it, seems more urgent to me in this place than it ever did before. As a matter of fact (and we'll talk about it later) it's precisely on this subject of the cogency and gravity of this fundamental attitude (I've learned all too well!) that a lack of conviction exists here, extending all the way up to the summit of authority. In other words, nobody here seems to realize the depth and clarity of the change in perspective which we are undergoing.—(The fact that this blind spot in the Church is the root cause of the universal dissatisfaction with religion is a card I haven't played yet—I'm waiting for the right moment.)—Man is in the process of crossing a new threshold; and people here flatter themselves that he is only going through a phase! At this moment, in the Church of God, this change lies at the heart of the problem of evangelization. It's not just a dispute over a thesis, but a real division in the way men think, on which an appropriate value judgment must be made.

The Curia is a strong modern building which backs onto some lovely gardens (palm trees, nectarine trees, mimosas) affixed to a cliff. The community (I'm with the "writers"—in other words, the archive mice lumped together with people from the Vatican Radio) is a motley one. It's like Chabanel (too much, perhaps) but places like this must be this way. Most people here are Spaniards, but there are a great many Germans, some Swiss, some Hungarians, an Irishman and an American. As I said before, everyone is very cordial and solicitous. But it's a little difficult to find anyone who speaks French or English.— Incidentally, I ran into Father Sebes, the Hungarian who was at Chabanel in 1940 and 1941. It seems that Fathers Charvet and Lichten and one or two others were released from prison in China, on condition that they leave the country immediately. I pity them. It will cost them dearly.

I have seen the "Great Chief" only once so far; and his frankness, directness and warmth immediately conquered me. I really feel that he will do all that he can to help me. But I also realize that if my book comes out, it will be interpreted as "a gesture of the Order," and I understand that it must therefore be examined with unusual care before any permission to publish is granted. Before a decision is taken, we are waiting for two final critical revisions from Louvain. Here, it's curiously like being in China. Nobody hurries.

As ever in Christ,
TEILHARD

Rome, October 30, 1948

Dear Friend,

I received your long letter of the 26th which brought me great pleasure and interested me very much. By all means hold to your decision to press on with your research in Paris and put off until later your projected visit to America. The delay will only make your trip more useful when the time comes. By the way, everything you wrote me about the structure of microscopic living particles is fascinating. I suppose it was with the electronic microscope that they first became visible? You'll have to tell me about it.

This is to confirm for you the date of my return. I've made a reservation on the train that leaves Rome on November 6, at 7 in the morning. It should bring me into Paris on the 7th before noon, but I'm not sure of the exact time. All this is not to tell you that I finally know my fate here. The second revision (much more intelligent, and a conclusion *for* the publication) has arrived, led me to clarify again certain points, and above all to add four final pages (good ones, I think) on the place of Evil in an evolving world. But will it be accepted in this new form, and when will I know? I have no idea. Meanwhile, the decision about the Collège de France will have to be made at the beginning of next week. The atmosphere is as promising as possible. So I feel perfectly philosophic about the whole business. Why shouldn't I? Basically, the game is won. It is only sad and funny to see here, everywhere about me, professors and officials continuing to repeat among themselves (with a semiconscious ignorance or an embattled complacency) that, in the opinion of scholars, "evolution is still not a proven fact"—the word "Evolution" being a semi-magic expression with which all the modern perspectives implied in the idea that the world (above all the human world) is not a stable thing, rush in pell-mell.—Once again, the old conflict between stability and movement! We'll talk about this later. Just lately a most influential Cardinal, Ruffini, (a *papabile*) from Sicily has published a popular book *against Evolution* (just as Saliège, Suhard and Liénard, but from the other end of the spectrum). All this has no importance, except to the degree that it helps me to appreciate the problem better. Christianity will move forward only when it has been converted to Humanity, i.e., to the Sense of the Human. As I am always saying, it's this habit of refusing to recognize the forward (*En*

Avant) motion of history which makes the Church sterile right now.—Admittedly though (as I told you), in this Roman and Catholic Christianity, the sense one has of the upward pull (the *En Haut*) is unique and breathtaking, if only we know how to use it properly. What brings this to my mind is a curious book called *Escape from Freedom*,* a psychoanalytic essay about human social anxiety which I've been reading recently. It's very interesting, but it betrays the old tendency of psychoanalysts to try to explain everything in terms of the play of certain inhibitions, without making any room for man's positive aspirations toward fulfillment (a fulfillment that can only be brought about by Something above but complementary to man). As if the internal "pull" were less scientific than the external "push"! In this kind of thinking, in fact, we see the Lamarckian-Darwinian pseudo-conflict reappearing in the field of psychoanalysis. (I intend to write a few pages about this for Maryse Choisy's journal.) In the end it's in terms of this ascensional "pull" that Christianity gives (or could give) the answer to the problem which bewilders Erich Fromm.

Apropos of books, if you can lay your hands on Carlo Levi's *Christ Stopped at Eboli* (there is a French translation), do so. As an analysis of peasant life, it's quite remarkable.

I continue to visit various corners of Rome and little by little see a good number of people. Yesterday at the Procure Saint-Sulpice I was presented to Garrigou-Lagrange. We smiled and talked about Auvergne. I also saw the Beauroys. I'll dine with them tomorrow. Father Arnou was visibly disappointed at not having caught you at Ste.-Geneviève the day you left for the Midi. He is extremely attached to you, and faithful. Charvet is still here. Tonight we dine at the Procure Saint-Sulpice.

I must finish quickly, if I'm to make the Saturday mail.

> With deep affection,
> TEILHARD

---

*Erich Fromm, Rinehart, N.Y., 1941.

LETTERS FROM MY FRIEND TEILHARD

Tomorrow is the feast of Christ the King. O, Rue Labrousse!—
Remember me to Françoise.* Yesterday at the forum, I thought
of her before the church of St. Frances of Rome. I wanted to go
in, in remembrance, but it was closed.

TEILHARD AND "THE TRIUMPHAL CHURCH"

*Teilhard returned to Paris empty-handed. His trip to Rome
resulted neither in the authorization to publish his book nor in
permission to press his candidacy for the Collège de France. But
as he took up his activities at the Rue Monsieur, far from re-
treating into gloomy solitude, he courageously returned to
work.*

*In early 1949, he heard by letter that Rome refused permis-
sion for the publication of* The Phenomenon of Man. *At about
the same time, Jean Piveteau, who held the chair of paleontology
at the Sorbonne, asked my friend to give a series of lectures to
his students. The subject, "The Meaning and Place of Man in
Nature," was one that pleased Teilhard. In early 1949, Teilhard
gave his first lecture—the completed series of which was to appear after his death in a little book published in Paris under the
title* Le Groupe Zoologique Humain.

*Immediately after the first lecture, illness drove Teilhard
back to the hospital on the Rue Oudinot. This time it was not
his heart that failed him, but his lungs. He had contracted a bad
case of pleurisy. This illness was, however, not as serious as the
last had been. His hospital stay was brief. It was followed by a
convalescence in the same rest home of the sisters of the Immaculate Conception at Saint-Germain where Teilhard had been in
1947. It was spring when he arrived. The nearby forest was just
budding and covered with a haze of green. During the month of
May I visited him often. I used to come just after his afternoon
rest period and together we would take a short walk, always
ending at the tearoom facing the forest.*

*Madame Françoise Raphael, one-time neighbor of Teilhard and Leroy on Rue
Labrousse in Peking, in 1948, widowed and living in Paris.

There in that climate of peace he contemplated his fate, received visitors and wrote. In August, he went to rest at his brother's house in Auvergne, and in September returned to Etudes.

Externally, things did not improve. In 1950, when I went briefly to America to continue my own work, he wrote to me that the attitude of Rome was stiffening. Msgr. Feltin, the archbishop of Paris, who had just returned from there, came privately to visit Etudes. *He had received his orders for the preachers who were to speak in churches during Lent. There were, he said, to be "three burning subjects"—Communism, evolutionism and Thomism. When one spoke of the first two, one must be against them; when one spoke of the third, one must be for it. It seemed a sure sign that some doctrinal document (whose subject was still a matter of conjecture) was about to be issued. But for the moment, nothing more was said.*

Such warnings, however, did not stop Catholic scholars in France from keeping their co-religionists posted on new developments in learning. A scientific symposium held later that year at Saint-Séverin was a great success. Professors Piveteau and Tintant were most effective. As for Teilhard, when he was invited to take the floor, he, too, spoke his "little piece" on "The Modern Idea of Evolution" impressively. Since he was still hoping against hope for the eventual publication of his Book No. 2*, he added that "I rather avoided the question of Adam."

Soon afterwards, the Cité Universitaire offered him the opportunity of speaking there. His subject was to be the Earth considered as "a living planet," whose human and whose superhuman function could be invoked to give a rational answer to the challenge of atheism. For Teilhard, the only way of refuting contemporary atheism was to recognize "that with the end of neolithic thinking . . . we have stopped imagining God as some kind of Great Proprietor or Master Builder," and begun to think about Him as the Love at the Heart of Reality.

I understand why critics may have been annoyed or even

**Le Groupe Zoologique Humain.*

scandalized by some of Teilhard's expressions. Language has its limitations. But how else was he to express his "new way of seeing" than by such words? In those days many people (a good number of Christians among them) still thought of creation, as finished and immutable, even though many more advanced minds were no longer comfortable with this notion. With the acceptance of the idea of general evolution growing more common, everything changed drastically.

Creation is an ongoing process. It continues its development in time and space. It is constant genesis, whose goal is the appearance of reflection and whose crown is spiritualization. This progressive movement is willed and animated by an Absolute Liberty—"the Super-Soul," as Teilhard called it, "of cosmogenesis" and "the Ultimate Ground of all our action."

The world is, therefore, a vast dependent system of related contingencies. With this understood, this "Super-Soul of cosmogenesis" can only be found by reaching outside the circle of phenomena, in other words, in the revelation of the existence of Something greater than we are ourselves.

Teilhard's originality lies in his belief that the work of evolution is the fruit of God's Love. To him, Love is the ultimate source of energy.

The round of conferences, meetings with friends and visits continued at its accustomed pace throughout the first six months of 1950. After his demobilization in 1919, Teilhard had made it a habit to leave his laboratory or office at about five o'clock in the afternoon. He then tried to spend time with people outside his religious circle in an attempt to discover what they were thinking and feeling. It was in these encounters with the "gentile" world that Teilhard came to understand modern problems. Before sitting down to write a memoir or a note, he felt he needed to be as knowledgeable as possible of these questions, so that he could speak freely and to the point. On many occasions I heard him discuss things which I felt were far beyond the understanding of his listeners. When I told him he was wasting his time, he answered that, quite on the contrary, he felt

it necessary to expose the reflections born of his personal medi-
tations before minds different from his own. In a letter to me on
March 31, 1950, he re-explained his method. "My interest now,"
he wrote, "lies in testing the value and sharpening the point of
those ideas you already know so well."

When Rome refused to give him permission for the publication of a second book on Man containing the series of six lectures he had prepared but not completely delivered at the
Sorbonne in 1949 ("The Human Zoologic Group"), Teilhard
wrote me that "this well-meaning but rather unintelligent Roman criticism makes me think the book can do with some retouching." With the help of Father René d'Ouince, he reworked
his manuscript. At that time, a bit pessimistically, he was dread-
ing, in his own words, "a Super-Censure." As it happened, his
presentiment turned out to be well-founded. The book did not
appear in his lifetime."

Teilhard's pessimistic outlook at the time was reinforced by
what he knew by hearsay about the attitude of high Vatican authorities. "It seems," he wrote, "that somebody at the Curia
wants the skin of a French theologian. It would be quite a victory for the integrists at this moment when they're thinking of defining the Assumption as a dogma!"

Teilhard took the announcement of so solemn a definition
very seriously. Not that he was in any way blind to the enormous importance of the Marial Mystery to the history of humanity. But he had so little confidence in the Roman method of
"pure mental deduction" which he was sure would be invoked
to support it, that he was distressed. To say, for example, "God
is, by definition, incorruptible; Our Lady gave birth to the God-
Man; therefore Our Lady is incorruptible" is only syllogistic
mindplay. If the definition of the dogma were to rest on such a
basis, it would, he felt, reduce the grandeur and universality of
Mary's role in the economy of salvation to a concept that could
easily be dealt with by human reason.

In Rome at that time another project, too, was being stud-
ied. In 1864, Pope Pius IX had published a Syllabus of Errors,

i.e., a list of erroneous doctrinal and philosophical propositions which he officially condemned. In 1950, there were rumors that another Syllabus was being prepared, but one that would be specifically addressed to the Fathers of the Society of Jesus. Its appearance would be a cruel blow to Teilhard's brothers in religion as well as to himself. He awaited it with trepidation.

CANDIDACY FOR THE ACADEMY OF SCIENCES

The geologists of Paris had always displayed an open admiration for the scientific work which had been done in China with the energy and participation of Teilhard. In 1950, a representative member of the scientific community, Prof. Charles Jacob, "took the unexpected initiative" of inviting him to stand as a candidate for full membership in the Institut de France, replacing René Maire.

Though not particularly enthusiastic at the prospect, because it meant that some of his supporters would have to withdraw votes pledged to another candidate whom he admired, Teilhard, urged by his friends to stand before he was too old, agreed to let his name be placed in nomination. He did it with the "vague impression that I'm doing something weak in giving in." On May 22, he was elected a full nonresident member.

Despite his hesitation, however, once he became an academician, Teilhard hoped he would have greater liberty for "launching new philosophical projectiles." But the years that followed were no easier for him than those which had gone before. Rome continued to be uneasy with his influence and to wish him far away. A new and permanent exile was being prepared for him—an exile from which he would only be allowed to revisit Paris once, and one in which he would end his days, far away from all he loved.

But even during the moments of doubt that 1950 brought, Teilhard was sustained by something that transcended worry about the machinations of his superiors in Rome. As much as ever, he was driven by the need to communicate his faith in an

"Evolver-God," and to inspire in others what he called the "Thirst for Life." Early in that year, he wrote me that he had given a conference in which he once again emphasized how irreplaceable to human progress was a "Thirst for Life."

The "Thirst for Life"—what did he mean by it? Surely, it was not some complacent optimism, some satisfaction with contact with creatures, some sort of higher epicureanism in which one tasted the joys of living in a world where every need was answered. Thus understood, this "Thirst for Life" would be a "contra-verity," unacceptable in any Christian context.

Teilhard's conception of the "Thirst for Life" was a quite different one. "Hominisation," he once wrote, "released an immense force on the world." This force set out to realize its potential to the degree that a "passion for the Whole" lifts it out of elementary egoism and helps increase the "growth of consciousness" in general evolution. Thus understood, and sustained by the profound movement of Matter rising up toward Spirit, this "Thirst" becomes a virtue.

But there is more. In the essay of November 1950, in which Teilhard examined this subject more deeply, he extended the action of this "Thirst" (without which the tendency of all things to converge or "centrate" on each other is inexplicable) to the whole mass of living matter. Because Man is reflective, because he is conscious of his potentialities, he above all does not escape this fundamental drive. In him, the "Taste for Life can only be a faith." The certainty that he is not imprisoned by the matter which is his individual matrix, that there is a way out, that there is light and air and love somewhere beyond death is a need which can only be described as absolute. "We must have such a faith," he wrote, "if only to save us from being stifled by the stuff of our being."

At first glance, all this may seem more intellectual than practical. But let us think a bit. From the moment that we understand the role that the will plays in bending the forces of nature toward a certain defined goal (however humble our tasks may be), the better we can see our responsibility to cooperate with the movement which pulls us forward. Action, coupled with a positive kind of resignation, justifies our effort. Without diminishing either our physical or moral suffering, it encourages us to "return" everything to God. To Teilhard's way of thinking, the maturation of the human world will be, in great part, the fruit of man's own efforts. The final attainment of God as much presupposes the work of self-stripping and detachment as the purification of water demands enrichment and aeration.

All through 1950 Teilhard's personal life remained at an impasse. There was still no news from Rome about the publication of his (he insisted) "purely scientific Human Zoologic Group lectures ("my Book No.2"), even though all the material for making such a decision had been on the Father General's desk since early May. Just the same, Etudes *held a reception to celebrate Teilhard's election to the Academy of Sciences and "more than 40 people came."*

Aside from this little bit of light and joy filtering through the gloom, the religious situation in France in general was unhappy. In July five Jesuits, most of them professors of theology at Lyon, were quietly dismissed. Out mutual friend, the philosophy teacher, Pierre St. Seine, also came under close scrutiny. His teaching at the scholasticate, bearing on biology, was declared suspect by the authorities, and he was ordered to send complete texts of his discourses to Rome. At about the same time an anonymous (and highly critical) little book called The Redemptive Evolution of Père Teilhard de Chardin *had appeared—altogether a bad sign for Teilhard's future.*

Nor were these his only disappointments at that time. Another one-time friend and colleague, Maurice T., a priest who had completely disappeared after the war's end, suddenly resurfaced. When we knew him first, he had been a young Jesuit in China, whom Teilhard thought sufficiently gifted to replace him as a paleontologist when the time came. He asked the authorities to return him to France to undertake specialized studies in the field. But with the German invasion, T. was mobilized and all the members of his family were killed in one bombard-

ment. In complete despair, he left the religious life. In 1949, Teilhard came across an address for him. He wrote at once. The letter went unanswered.

In 1949, the Maoist forces took Peking. In 1950, the Chinese revolution triumphed on the mainland, and missionaries were expelled, dispersed or imprisoned. The same year, the Korean War broke out, and all of Eastern Asia seemed to be turning into a powder keg. Teilhard's attempt to find some news of Pei Wen-Chung, one-time pupil of the Abbé Breuil and Teilhard's collaborator at Choukoutien, all came to nothing. Another friend, a geologist named Eddie Bien, had sent him word that he had left China and moved with his family to California. But where were all the rest? What had become of them? Teilhard knew nothing of their fate. Only the faithful Wong Wen-Hao arranged to see him during a trip he made to Europe close to New Year's Eve.

THE BOOK ON MAN REJECTED

Just as in 1949, Rome had finally made her judgment clear on the question of publishing Teilhard's book The Phenomenon of Man. *Despite Teilhard's retouching and correcting, the manuscript was rejected on the grounds that, in the eyes of the censors, "it went beyond the bounds of science properly described."*

Both the caution to silence and a new demand that he renounce his mission made life an agony for Teilhard. But once more his courage and his strength of character held firm. He remained faithful and obedient, complaining only occasionally at the rigidity of a decision that was unintelligible to him. In this spirit, he continued privately with the writing of his works.

He was profoundly convinced of the truth of his position. All his letters are shot through with the same driving idea: unless the Church invites mankind to develop its human powers, she will not regain its interest. And this is a challenge she must meet, no matter how painful the effort.

LETTERS FROM MY FRIEND TEILHARD

All year long, Teilhard continued to explore his ideas. He wrote a letter to Jaime Torres-Bodet, director-general of UNES-CO, which institution had just issued a formal statement on "The Equality of Races." Though no one appreciated the sanctity and worth of every human life better than did Teilhard, he objected to any definition that grouped all the branches of humanity in one homogeneous mass. Especially from a biological point of view, the error in the UNESCO proclamation was quite clear. All animal groups, including man, develop by subdividing in such a way that they find their identity, not in uniformity, but in their complementary aspect. At about the same time, Teilhard received another commendation from the French Assistant in Rome. It was just "a splash of holy water," he complained. Nothing more. Happily, however, the dreaded Syllabus did not yet appear. For the moment at least, Teilhard and his friends could breathe easily. In early July, an article by the Goncourt Prize-Winner, André Billy, presented Teilhard and his ideas most enthusiastically once again before a sophisticated secular readership.

That August as always, Teilhard went back to Moulins, to the chateau of his brother Joseph. In the calm of the countryside, he set out to write an essay studying his own psychological journey from his conventional childhood religiosity at war with his strong attraction to material permanence, to the understanding of his maturity in which both elements were reconciled. He called his essay "Le Coeur de la Matière," and in it he explored how in his own life he had had the experience summed up in the phrase in his letter of August 18, 1950: "The fact of God changes before our eyes."*

---

*Teilhard was well aware of the danger of misinterpretation to which such a statement lends itself and treated it at greater length in his long essay "Accomplir l'Homme," which was published by Editions Grasset (1968). He also wrote about the subject to a friend: "The vague feelings of my youth have now been swallowed by an immense Energy . . . not of a 'God Who is dead,' as Nietzsche says, but of a 'God Who changes,' to the extent (as I'm now in the habit of saying) that the *En Haut* is now inextricably joined to the *En Avant* that religions never took into account before." P.L.

THE ENCYCLICAL HUMANI GENERIS

But very soon, the country calm of his vacation was profoundly troubled. Toward the end of August, Pope Pius XII released his Holy Year Encyclical "Humani Generis." In the solitude of Moulins, Teilhard did not have access to a copy of the text and had to rely on summaries in the newspaper for information.

As always, his first reflex was obedience and submission. Although they had no proof, many people believed that the document was directed specifically against Teilhard's own theories. My friend never said anything to indicate that he thought this was so (though he did sometimes seem edgy about the document) and he never behaved as though he saw himself as singled out for criticism. He gladly recognized whatever was positive in the papal pronouncement, such as its "approbation of scholars researching the origins of man as having risen from preexistent, living matter." In point of fact, given that at the time the encyclical was issued Evolution was still suspect in the Church, that statement represented some small progress.

But because of the influence that encyclicals had in those days to Christians and especially to Catholics, one must admit that Teilhard sometimes criticized it rather sharply. His reaction is understandable. With a passion such as he had for the recognition of an "ever-greater Christ" (i.e., a Christ Who could be better known and loved if the preeminent role He plays in history as in the evolution of the world were better understood) Teilhard dearly wished to see the Church put its spiritual power at the service of propagating this role. He was anxious to see the Church move away from the juridical approach it so often displayed, to see it employ a new and clearer language adapted to modern men and thus to reveal the Object of Faith more clearly to Christians and non-Christians alike that led him to employ the vigorous terms he did in analyzing the papal document.

LETTERS FROM MY FRIEND TEILHARD

PROCLAMATION OF THE DOGMA
OF THE ASSUMPTION

Of Teilhard's sincere devotion to Our Lady, there can be no doubt. To his mind, Mary was not only the young Jewish girl called to be the Mother of Christ; she was also an essential element in his Christianity. He admitted the Assumption of the Virgin without hesitation. But the possible wording of its official declaration troubled him. As he so often said, in order to better appreciate this Mystery, as well as all the others in the Deposit of Faith, language had to change.

In its energy and strength, Teilhard's letter of August 29, 1950, is a fine example of his style and verve. Hardly a polemic, it represents the reaction of a Christian ever more at ease in expressing what he thinks, in that he feels it his duty to show to those who have not yet seen it, the new Face of Christ.

By then Teilhard saw the possibility of a new chance to do field work. After the discovery of the Australopithecine sites in South Africa, his reputation as a specialist in the geologic layers of the Upper Tertiary and Quaternary drew anthropologists on the terrain to ask for his participation. The idea of a trip there genuinely interested him. He discussed it with his old friend, George Barbour, one-time professor at Yenching University in Peking, when the latter came to visit at Moulins.

The idea of a trip to Africa had been growing in Teilhard's mind since 1946. By late 1950, he had definitely made up his mind to go there by July of the following year.

While he waited, he wrote (and sent to Rome) a note offering a scientific objection to the concept of monogenesis.* It is irreconcilable with what we know from biology that our human species should be descended from a single pair. In nature, everything happens in terms of "populations"—a word which denotes a group of individuals whose genetic resources constitute

---

*"Monogénisme et Monophylétisme, une distinction essentiel à faire," 10 Octobre 1950, Paris.

a pool, a stock whose genes are not prearranged but mixed. From this pool, through the play of sexual combinations, are born new types which serve as points of departure for the formation of species. This is a universal law. The concept of "monophylism," therefore, Teilhard explained, makes infinitely better sense than "monogenism" as an approach to human origins. A phylum is a "reality ... of dynamic nature which must without question be classified among the natural unities of the world." Man belongs to a phylum. Whereas monogenesis is inconceivable, in terms of modern biology, monophylogenesis is not. That note to Rome, like so many others, went unanswered.

MORE PROBLEMS WITH AUTHORITY

In a letter written on November 11, 1950, Teilhard refers to some lectures he gave in Liège and Brussels with the comment, "I'm quite worn out—I wonder what Rome will think of them." This constant preoccupation with not displeasing his superiors is characteristic of Teilhard. His spiritual adventure drew him to an ever-stronger attachment to the Church. At the same time, his passion for Christ, his friendship with others in the scientific community, the difficulty so many people had in accepting the official formulae the Church imposed—all these things pressed him to say what he was thinking frankly and without anger.

But in Rome, at the time, there was little peace. The integrists there were baffled by the fact that the encyclical turned out to be such a fiasco when it appeared in France. Efforts to develop and propagate the major ideas of the pontifical pronouncement met with small success. At the end of the year, a meeting of religious orders at the Vatican, to which Father d'Ouince was invited, gave the Father General the opportunity to chasten the intellectuals of the Society of Jesus for laxity in the defense of the document. The report made by a Father Visitor who came to investigate the French scholasticates in 1948, which had been responsible for the dismissals at Fourvière and the removal of the books of criticized theologians, still left a resi-

due of considerable anger in Rome. An article in Etudes *that falls on the encyclical by Robert Rouquette was judged "inadequate."*

Eternal optimist that he was, Teilhard declared these developments need not be taken too tragically, since all progress— even in the spiritual order—was inevitably accompanied by strife and shock. Evolution on the human level as well as on every other level never happens without work and suffering. It is not enough to let oneself be borne passively along by it; man must collaborate in the event. This bitter truth was one that Teilhard understood too well.

Paris, March 31, 1950

Dear Friend,

... Here we are enjoying a soft and delicious spring, with greening chestnut trees and pink fruit trees along the Champs Elysées, just as they used to bloom in old Peking. In my life now, the most important news is that the Roman criticism of my Book No. 2 (which, it seems, was mislaid for three weeks in one of Father Goussault's desk drawers) has finally arrived. It's unintelligent, of course, but well meaning, and only asks that I touch up some details (dotting the i's a bit)—a thing that I've just finished. But will it satisfy them? Or will there be a sort of "Super-Censure" which will sink the project once and for all? In any case, all the materials are in now. I can only wait.

Apart from this, I gave five lectures at the Sorbonne (an elective course to be credited toward the students' degree in anthropology) on the Pleistocene of the Far East, as well as a conference at the Cité Universitaire, about my "hobby," "the Ultra-Human." I did, however, give the subject a new form and called it "The Stages of a Living Planet." (Which reminds me—You should have received a copy of the first part of an answer I wrote for André George on "What Is Life?" in the *Nouvelles Littéraires*.)—A meeting on evolution at St. Severin, in which Dubarle and d'Ouince had asked me to participate along with Piveteau and Tintant, and with Dubarle as Chairman was quite successful. In any case, d'Ouince is delighted. Nobody broke any eggs! Last week at Grassé's there was an international symposium on the sociology of animals, which Emerson and Allee, two professors from Chicago, attended. It was a real success. St. Seine is back from Mongre. On the other hand, the literary sociologists from the Sorbonne *glitter* by their absence! I wonder how long they will keep on treating man as though he were a cosmos unto himself, unrelated to the rest of creation, just as the theologians do . . .

Doncoeur's health is now much better. But he's still not back from the Rue Oudinot. Rouquette has returned from a pilgrimage to Rome without having gotten overly sentimental. He isn't very clear about what's going on there. From what he says, though, we gather that somebody at the Holy Office is after the skin of a French theologian. Also it seems that they're thinking of making a dogma of the Assumption, without any historical consideration and as a pure mental deduction from Mary's Divine Maternity! To quote Bonsirven* the really interesting thing about all this is that it establishes quite clearly the fact that Revelation is a continuing process. Furthermore, it looks (perhaps) as though they finally will publish a Syllabus, *intra societatem* (in which case the Company would serve as a guinea pig) if not *urbi et orbi. Si non e vero . . .* !**—As to Du Parc, I don't have the latest news, but I'm sure he'll need a long rest after his pleurisy. I didn't see Lejay last Thursday. But he is certainly thriving.

Last Tuesday I dined with the director of the Sureté (!), an old Normalien, and very nice, too, at the Place Beauveau. Next week I'm going to an almost tête-à-tête dinner with Joliot-Curie at Madame René Mayer's (the cabinet minister's wife). The thing that draws, or rather interests me in these situations is the

---

*A Jesuit scripture professor of Teilhard's acquaintance.
**. . . e ben trovato. (Italian expression to the effect that at least it makes a good story. Lit. If it is not true, it is a good invention. (M.L.)

opportunity they give for testing the value and sharpening the point of the ideas that you know so well.

The Marshall Field you mention in your letter is probably the uncle of my friend Henry Field.... A powerful man is always good to know.

Very affectionately yours,
TEILHARD

Paris, April 19, 1950

Dear Friend,

For two days now I've tried without success to find a moment to answer your long letter of the 12th. Since Easter my time has been literally eaten up, and not always very usefully. Oh, well!...

I wanted, however, to answer your questions quickly.—Yes, I understand the pain of isolation that you speak of and how it can be aggravated by the suspicion that we perhaps commit a psychological and mystical error in seeking the Divine in a pure state, outside of all material contact. I imagine that many priests right now are undergoing this dark (and hopefully) fruitful suffering.—A new humano-Christian mysticism can only be an extension of the old. Nothing else will serve. Meanwhile, I can only offer you my own method of dealing with the problem: Love Christ *fortiter* (the ever-greater Christ) *through men*, and (if I dare say it) even beyond the hierarchical Church. And, in order to adore and to discover this greater conception of Divinity, vow yourself to serve the further development of humanity through research. The silent workings of Providence will do the rest. But, above all, hold high the spirit of adventure and of conquest, as Whitehead says ...

... Here there's nothing substantially new. I still have had no answer from Rome to the proposed corrections to my Book No. 2, which were reviewed by d'Ouince and passed on at Easter by the French Assistant. I'll wait till the end of the month for a reaction. And while I wait, I'll write my lecture for the Cité Universitaire on "The Phases of a Living Planet." This keeps me busy. But once it's given, what will I do with it?

St. Seine is back and everyone is very busy about the Catholic Intellectuals Week, in which I am not planning to take part, except for one little meeting on the Rue Madame. Jouve had to go back for a while to the Rue Oudinot, to the very room where I was last year and Doncoeur this last winter. Largely it's a question of nervous spasms. Du Parc, however, is not too strong. He's still at Saint-Germain before leaving for a long rest at home. . . .

. . . I must stop now so I can get this letter out more quickly. If I've forgotten something, it will keep for the next time.

> Affectionately always,
> TEILHARD

Paris, May 14, 1950

Very Dear Friend,

. . . Now to move on to news of Paris. Nothing new as far as I'm concerned (still no response to the corrected manuscript* sent to Rome to Gorostarzu at Easter!) except that, following a totally unexpected initiative taken by Jacob, for two weeks now I've been a candidate for the Institute (a candidate to be a non-resident member in the mineralogy section, replacing the botanist Maire from Algiers). Hence the delay in answering your letter. What is proposed really amounts to a candidacy *in extremis*, in which I find myself, quite against my will, competing with Guyénot from Geneva, for whom I have a great esteem. Guyénot is supported by Caullery, who would ordinarily be for me. The election is in ten days. Many of the people at the Acade-

---

*Le Groupe Zoologique Humain.

my support me, but quite a few votes have already been committed to Guyénot. If I don't make it this time, I imagine the affair will be put off for three more months, until Cotton leaves a vacant place. I'm really not very enthusiastic about presenting my candidacy immediately. But the insistence of my friends (from d'Ouince on down) has decided me. I have the vague impression that in acting now I'm doing something weak by giving in.

As well you know, this place at the Institute only interests me to the extent that it will protect me against certain attacks, or, to make another comparison, to the degree where it will give me a platform from which I can launch my "projectiles." And speaking of ideas, it seems to me that with the help of God I still haven't finished contributing everything I'm capable of giving. Even when nothing new comes to my mind, this or that old intuition often takes so crowning a position that the whole of the old thought structure beneath it is almost entirely renewed. One of the things I'm thinking about now is the evidence that the (fruitful, I think) unease which agitates the Christian or even the non-Christian world around us is caused not so much by some change "in theological studies" as by a change in "the face of God" as we perceive it. It's neither more nor less than this. This change from the conception of "Father-God" to "Evolver-God" is based less on the fact (or the coincidence) of our historical passage from a neolithic to an industrial age than it is based on our consciousness of having passed from the conception of an aggregate Cosmos to the conception of an organic cosmos-in-genesis. I realize I'm expressing myself very clumsily and abstractly. But I feel the difference so intensely. It's like moving from ice into fire.

Catholic Intellectuals Week has come and gone again—much too crowded with lecturing by literary and theological types, as always. I've come to the conclusion that there can be no valuable thought (not even religious thought) any more, without a restructuring of our idea of matter (physics, biology—"Science"). Nevertheless, everyone feels the week went off quite well. I had no part in it, except for one meeting where we selected speakers for the day devoted to biology. It gave me the occasion once more to emphasize the absolute irreplaceability of the "Thirst for Life" (and of its necessary condition, the irreversibility of reflectivity, of course) in the process of Biogenesis once it has reached the human stage. St. Seine spoke brilliantly. . . .

. . . Last Thursday the Archbishop came to dine with us, absolutely in private. He made a fine impression, and the contact between him and the *house* was very sympathetic. He's not an intellectual, but he's a man of great good will. He understands the weakness of the Roman position and he only asks to advise us. . . .

. . . Let me see whether Jouve wants to use the end of this page to add a note. He seems in quite good spirits now.

Courage.

My warm affection,
TEILHARD

Paris, June 25, 1950

Dear Friend,

. . . Things are very much the same here. But I sometimes ask myself how long the calm can last. Rome still has not answered me, though, since the beginning of May; all the materials for a decision have been on the Father General's desk. There's something a little ominous about the silence. Did I tell you that in *Osservatore Romano* of June 1, Cardinal Ruffini, the *"papabile"* archbishop of Palermo, wrote an article, something of a resume of his book of two years ago, warning Catholics, especially French Catholics, of the danger of extending evolution too generally toward man? The cardinal is still persuaded that evolution implies that God breathed a soul into the body of an ape. *Irisio gentilium,* as I wrote to Gorostarzu. Also, and incidentally, the Librairie du Cèdre (Pensée Catholique) has announced the publication of an anonymous little book called *The Redemptive Evolution of Pére Teilhard de Chardin!* At least they should have called it *Evolving Redemption*, as I wrote to Gorostarzu. In any case, all this will certainly not help me straighten out my problems!

We're all waiting for July to hear the decisions of the Holy Office concerning the "New Theology." D'Ouince is as optimistic as ever. He comforts both himself and me with hope that I'll get an *Imprimatur* once this storm is over and it's clear that I am not included among the people it condemns. . . . Meanwhile, we hear it said quite openly that five professors from Fourvière have been quietly dismissed. As somebody said recently (jokingly, but seriously), thinking freely in the Church these days means going underground. Come to think of it, that is what I've been doing for thirty years.

All this is fairly disagreeable, but not really disturbing. It is so clearly evident that "the wall has been breached" around the "old-fashioned" Christianity, and that from now on no one will be able to understand the Supernatural except as the basis and as a prolongation of the "Ultra-Human."

St. Seine has just been asked to send to Rome the texts of his courses. Of course, he sent an excised version. But will he get away with it? He doesn't seem particularly distressed, and he continues to work very well at the museum.—In that connection, did I tell you that on the occasion of my candidacy at the Institute, Lucien Cuénot wrote me the kindest letter—half pleasant, half sad, but very touching in its trembling handwriting, and in its closing with the P.S.: "All the same, think of me in your prayers." Evidently, he feels he's coming to his end. . . .

. . . Two Mondays ago here at *Etudes* we had a champagne party for the Academicians. More than forty people came, and those who did not sent regrets. It's quite clear now that I was named to the Institute less for my science than for my ideas—an infinitely more interesting development. Of course, I'm letting Rome know all about it. . .

. . . Edouard Petit just arrived, after having left Tientsin in April. One after the other, everyone is coming home (Denis is in Japan) and no one can go back. I wrote to Pei (the letters crossed between Hong Kong and Canton) for news, asking him to go and see Vetch to find out what became of our Geobiology publications. This very morning I heard from E. Bien, who's still happy with his oil company job in California, where he lives with his wife and son.

I'll write more soon. (Still nothing from Rome about the book, despite the two letters to Gorostarzu . . . Things are looking worse and worse.)

Affectionately as ever,
TEILHARD

Paris, July 6, 1950

Very Dear Friend,

. . . Nothing really new here. Chaillet* has just returned from Rome, very proud of his Holy Year pilgrimage, which, it seems, left him with a strong impression of what French Catholicism is. But he had neither the time (nor the taste) to see influential people, even the Father General. At Rome, they're really talking now about a Syllabus. And, at the same time, there's a rumor that the whole thing is just a bugaboo from which they are pulling back now, because their goal, the official dispersion of the new theology, has been attained.—No guarantee, though.—Meanwhile, the dismissal of de Lubac continues to create a certain backwash. He is circulating letters of protest. The vaunted Syllabus (if it does come out) is expected to appear at the end of the month or in August. In any case, at vacation time.

I just realized that I haven't told you that I did receive, though Goussault,* an answer from Rome regarding my Book

*Pierre Chaillet. Jesuit, founder of *Témoignage chrétien.* Hero of the French Underground during World War II.
*Jacques Goussault. Jesuit Paris Provincial 1948–54.

No. 2. It is "negative," naturally. They can't find any proposition for me to retract; they simply hide behind the reason that in this collection I pass beyond the bounds of "science," properly defined. That, of course, I formally dispute. Politely, but vigorously, I wrote to Gorostarzu calling his attention to the fact that the official Church has completely lost the ear of the world, that it no longer feels with it, and that churchmen in high places are yielding themselves up to a real intellectual Malthusianism. Now I'm busy stenciling my new book, as I did *The Phenomenon*—not in order to propagate it, but to preserve it. For the most part, I'll distribute it to my new confreres at the Institute, if only to affirm that it really does deal with "science." The question has arisen of an elective course "for advanced students" in paleontology at the Sorbonne, and Piveteau has asked me to collaborate on it. My plan is to use the occasion to complete a third writing of my views on "the Human" (its biological structure and physical nature), and to publish it (without revision or submission to the censors, naturally—it is my right) in the *Annals of Paleontology*, which Piveteau now wants to extend to subjects which are not strictly technical.

And now to finish with the "integrist" question. There's talk about an upcoming dismissal of two unnamed Dominicans (surely not Dubarle!) as well as the Jesuits. A Jesuit theodicy professor from Mongré (Father Thomas) has been prematurely sent away to make his tertianship, with some talk about his making his biennial year in Rome right afterward. St. Seine seems unharmed. The book *The Redemptive Evolution of Père Teilhard de Chardin* is now out. Its author is Louis Jugnet, a professor of philosophy in a high school in Toulouse. The book is inoffensive and weak. The author (usually a writer for *Pensée Catholique* and a notorious integrist) places me right beside the Existentialists and the Hindus. (Precisely my two *bêtes noirs!*) Impossible to be more wrong. Furthermore, none of my last *clandestines* are cited in the book; only the old classics. So, I'm in no danger . . .

. . . René Meyer just left my room. He sends you greetings. St. Seine thanks you very much for your letter; he's off for a week at Notre-Dame-des Neiges. As for me, I'll be here until August 15, and then to Auvergne.

Courage.

Affectionately,
TEILHARD

Paris, July 29, 1950

Very Dear Friend,

Where are we heading? I'm always such a bad prophet in the short run that I no longer pride myself on my prognostications. Still—however disconcerting this present schism between America and Asia is—I just can't force myself to take a pessimistic view of it. The forces of compression and unification operating on the earth are so intractable that they must have the final say. Furthermore, from the simple Christian point of view, the crust of fixity and inertia accumulated around the Church through 2,000 years of earthly sovereignty is so thick and paralyzing that one almost catches oneself hoping for some *shock* which will put the spirit of Christ back in circulation among the newborn waves of the universe.

Here my routine remains the same as ever. Because of recent conversations, I've written a new little clandestine called "To See More Clearly, or Reflections on Two Forms of Spirit." (It's about the spirit of centration vs. the spirit of diffusion.) I'll send it to you in September when I finish stenciling it. I find it very helpful to jot down this way a certain number of central points so as to have them on hand to give to people who want them as a reference after oral discussions. Yesterday, I couldn't restrain myself from sending two thick (but very amical) pages to Torres-Bodet pointing out to him the scientific uselessness as well as the practical danger of UNESCO's recent proclamation of the dogma on the equality of races. As if any zoological group

59

could appear and develop without branching constantly! Of course, it's not a question of "equality," but of "complementarity in convergence" (a "convergence" which does not exclude the momentary prominence of certain of its branches over others). If, as is likely, I give those "lectures for advanced students" on The Anatomy of the Human Group at the Sorbonne, I will take the opportunity to develop these delicate views publicly.

Nothing from Rome (except a splash of holy water from Gorostarzu). People are now saying that the famous "Syllabus" will not come out after all (whether it is because people in high places have felt the rising anger or because the dismissal of the professors of Fourvière is judged sufficient punishment). It is also said that the proclamation of the dogma of the Assumption will stay inside desk drawers.—Very recently, *La Civiltà Cattolica* (in two lead articles) has deigned to recognize that overpopulation will begin to be a problem (not before 75 years [*sic*]); and that the moment has come to see what the Church can do about it without approving birth control. "Colonies of virgins" and "currents of continence in marriage" were suggested. I cannot imagine how one could be more open about playing with the limits of psychological forces, or could depend more strongly on the power of a faith which one does everything one can to weaken. Actually, though, a germ of good sense and realism comes to light in the fact that it is explicitly recognized by the review that *crescite et multiplicamini* is no longer the supreme rule of sexual morality.

I must have told you that the integrist Libraire du Cèdre has brought out an anonymous little volume (written by one Jugné [*sic*], professor in a high school in Toulouse and a regular writer for *Pensée Catholique*) called *The Redemptive Evolution of P. Teilhard de Chardin*. It's not really dangerous, only my old clandestines are used—and badly. But the annoying thing is that I cannot seem to stop my friends from buying the book which advertises itself as "the first expose" of my celebrated clandestines. To top it off, the three stars, which are the hallmark of the series, have disappeared from the book; all one sees is my name.

No reaction from Rome, and with good reason. It seems they're going to let it drop.

As usual, I'll be going to Auvergne to my brother's house, leaving sometime between the 10th and the 15th of August. I'll stay a month; my mail will follow me.

. . . Nothing new at *Etudes*. I still don't know whether future Roman orders will change anything. Doncoeur is coming to dinner. Lejay made a tour of Brittany. St. Seine is here after a short vacation at Fleur-des-Neiges. Jouve is well enough. He is in good spirits, but he has so many different kinds of health problems! He's going to go home and take a rest in August. . . .

> Affectionately,
> TEILHARD

Les Moulins
par Neuville (Puy de Dôme), August 18, 1950

Dear Friend,

Your letter of the 12th just reached me here at my brother's house, where I'm exercising a vague kind of "chaplaincy," facing the chain of puys, far from the railroad and deep in a forest of oaks. I've been here for a week and plan to stay until the middle of September.

Of course there's nothing really new. I've tossed off a first sketch (I wonder if it will be definitive?) of an essay I've been thinking of writing for a long time. I'm calling it "Le Coeur de la Matière"* (not at all in the sense of Graham Greene!). In this essay, I'm reconstructing chronologically the psychological growth I've undergone since childhood, leading me from a vague and general sense of the cosmos to that which I now call "The Christique Sense."—At least they can't accuse me of writ-

---

*Finally published by Editions du Seuil in 1977.

ing philosophy this time! But doubtless, even so, the essay won't be publishable, due to the fact that the psychological testimony it carries is still the old refrain: "the face of God changes before our eyes . . . In order to be able to adore, we must have a new face for Him." Also, it's now finally announced that the dogma of the Assumption will be proclaimed November 1! In itself, this event doesn't displease me; I'm too convinced of the biopsychological necessity of the "Marial" (compensating for the masculinity of Jahweh in our piety) not to feel the profound need for such a gesture. But is it opportune to make the move at just this moment? What I mean is that given the limited language and resources of present theological thinking, will not the definition of the Assumption, as the masses will understand it, present a provocation and a challenge to physics and biology? I'm worried.—In such a case, is our only recourse to find our optimism hoping for the worst? Must we really sit and wait for the very clumsiness with which the official Church is about to affirm that she continues to live in a universe in which the rest of us do not, to be the shock that will reawaken the Christian conscience?—I almost hope so.

Did I tell you that in the *Figaro Littéraire* of July 5, André Billy of the Academy Goncourt published a "sensational" article on me in which he (dangerously) praised my clandestines, a little as though they were the germ of some new religion? . . . Some of my friends (notably Valensin) were very upset by this "pavé de l'ours"*. But I don't think it will make any trouble for me, because luckily, Billy only names three of my old essays ("Le Milieu Divin," "Comment Je Crois," "L'Esprit de la Terre")— he was sorry he couldn't get "L'Energie Humaine," so I've sent him a copy), and he expressly says they're very difficult to find. That's really all I need to clear me in the eyes of the authorities.—To tell the truth, though, I'm quite aware I'm not as inno-

---

*Reference to the gesture of the clumsy, well-intentioned Bear in the La Fontaine fable who attempted to brush a fly from the nose of a sleeping friend, and ended by flattening his skull. Moral: "Better a clever enemy than a foolish friend."(M.L.)

cent as all that. But how can I stop what I'm doing without failing in all my duties before God and man?. . . I have therefore decided to go on just as before, putting my trust in luck, or more exactly, in the legitimacy of my cause. I'm quite aware that all the heretics have said this, but generally their attitude was not directed toward further extending Christ's grandeur over everything. And this, fundamentally, is the only thing with which I can be reproached.

> Affectionately,
> TEILHARD

Les Moulins, August 29, 1950

Dear Friend,

Would you believe that George Barbour just passed 24 hours here (naturally he made sketches of the countryside in all directions!) just before taking the plane for America? (He had been in England on family business.) While he was here, he gave me all the information that I may need about Johannesburg and Pretoria. Now, we'll see about that.

Right now I am making my retreat quite peacefully in a house which has just regained its calm after two very busy weeks full of visits. More and more now, "making a retreat" is becoming an occasion for me to return myself to the presence of God. I simply cannot understand how people can still be satisfied with (much less carried away by) the "Exercises." Of course their schema is quite splendid. But the "cosmology" (and hence their Christology!) is so childish that it literally stifles me from beginning to end. What we need is a complete transposition of the Ignatian scheme in terms of organic universe (a growing universe) as we understand it today. I think such a transposition is perfectly possible, and sometime I may sketch one out. But who would want it? The problem with the "Exercises" only reflects in miniature the whole tragedy of the present-day Church.

LETTERS FROM MY FRIEND TEILHARD

Since my last letter, the second expected bombshell (other than the upcoming declaration of the Assumption) has exploded. Of course, I'm referring to the Encyclical. I've only seen the summaries in the papers, but on the other hand, the last ten days I've spent most of my time answering, orally or by letter, the S.O.S.'s which come to me from every side. In fact, except for the bother of having to show people how to interpret (or really make sense of) the words of the Encyclical, this famous document has left me quite calm. Just issuing a statement will not stop the world from turning. Still, it's rather vexing to know that what Rome wants to do (exalt Mary, keep dogma from evaporating into symbolism, and maintain a certain primacy and unity for man) *is absolutely right,* though in order to make people agree to these things, the Church must find another way to express herself.—Nor is it just a question of words (as the Encyclical would have one think). It's a question of an understanding of the World, because the World, from this time forward, has acquired a new dimension (genetic Organicity, to be precise), and such a growth in size transforms ideas—even though the Encyclical denies it. Say what they may, though, a sphere is not a circle!—On the whole, the document has a strong integrist flavor, especially marked in its condemnation of irenicism*.—As if the adjustment of our Christology (or rather the widening of it) to the quantitative and organic dimensions of our new world view were a question of making concessions!—I sometimes wonder whether in this year's Roman gestures, a good psychoanalyst might not discover clear traces of a specific religious perversion: an orthodoxy fraught with masochism and sadism, in which one actually takes pleasure in swallowing the truth, or making it swallowed, under its grossest and most stupid form. But perhaps I go too far!—Still, I assure you I do not feel the slightest bitterness or discouragement. I've simply decided to continue directly on my way down the path which seems to be directly

*Term used to describe peaceful and conciliatory method of dealing with Church matters, particularly in the field of Christian truth. The antonym of polemicism.

oriented toward the dogmatic realism that Rome desires and asks for. The thing with which I most reproach the Roman theologians is their attempt to keep our idea of Christ from growing (and thus keep men from adoring Him fully). They would certainly be astonished to hear anyone say this about them. Still, it is this that I feel so strongly, as do all those who are attached to my "clandestines."

Otherwise, nothing very new. I'm too isolated here to really know which way the wind is blowing . . .

. . . Courage.

Yours in deep and true affection,
TEILHARD

P.S.

Did you know that Barbour's married son, Ian, is working at Chicago on cosmic rays with Fermi?

Jouve is resting at Montélimar. I expect him back in Paris toward the beginning of October.

Paris, October 19, 1950

Very Dear Friend,

It seems an exorbitant length of time since I've written or heard from you—the proof that all is well . . .

. . . Nothing new in my life now, except that I am acting more and more as *if* I am going to leave for Johannesburg at the end of next July. This gives me an interest, a reason for being, and incidentally, provides a counter-irritant or "screen" to reassure the Roman high command, which I sense is getting a little "nervous" over me right now. It's nothing I can really put my finger on. I simply feel it in the air. The idea of seeing me disappear from the scene for a few months may help to ease a situation which, I must admit, I'm not doing much to ameliorate. My Book No.2 is being distributed (to specialists and colleagues only, notably those from the Institute). Its appearance was announced without much fuss in the synopsis of material available to members, and nobody at Rome reads that list—fortunately). Furthermore, exasperated by the nonsense which is being spouted even here on the question of monogenism, I decided to send a brief statement, from a purely objective point of view (I'll provide you with a copy), to Father de Gorostarzu with a pleasant but clear letter, calling to his attention that in contrast to the encyclical "Pascendi" (which was aimed at the people trying to undermine the glory of Christ), the encyclical "Humani Generis" (where one may search in vain for anything "human" as the word is understood today) was aimed at those who sought to enrich and intensify our understanding of the grandeur of Christ. What Rome did with this encyclical was to bombard its own front lines. I haven't yet had a reaction, and maybe I won't have one. I imagine that the poor Father General will receive a great many more such disagreeable reflections before all this is over.

Right now, on the 23rd and 24th, I'm going to Liège and Brussels (at the invitation of our Fathers there and with higher authorization) to give a lecture on the "Future of Humanity," as seen by a biologist. I'm not very enthusiastic about the prospect, but I imagine that it's a duty (and Monod* wrote this to me again yesterday) precisely like my plan to go to see the Australopithecines in Africa. How curious it is to think that we must actually struggle with the Church to be able to adore (to the point of satiety) that Christ which is hers to give by fact and by right! It's somewhat on this note (with a "Prayer to Christ Ever Greater") that my (unpublishable autobiographical) essay, "Le Coeur de la Matière" (not "The Heart of *the* Matter" in Graham Greene's sense, but "The Heart of *Matter*") will end. I finally finished it three months ago. (It's not very long, just about 50.)

As to the rest—everything at *Etudes* is as it always is, except that dear du Parc died gently of consumption at Saint-Germain. Jouve is very well, more petulant than ever. Lejay is flourishing

*Professor Theodore Monod, Biologist of the Academy of Sciences.

and influential. St. Seine made his trimester of teaching at Chantilly. Yesterday I dined with three people recently returned from Shanghai ... Everyone agrees that, in China, the time of European dominance is momentarily over. Aurora University** seems to have survived thanks to the Norman subtlety of Father de Germaine. But for how long? In contrast to Father Zupan (the Yugoslav from Sofia of whom I spoke to you last winter), the "Old Shanghaian" finds no heady perfume in Marxism. As he sees it, it's a case of "no breaks in the net where one is caught. The system is technically perfect" but stifling.

... I'm sure that I've forgotten something, but it will keep for next time.

Affectionately,
TEILHARD

Paris, November 11, 1950

Very Dear Friend,

... Forgive me for not having sent you the publications from the Institute of Geobiology. I only have *one* copy of the series, and the study of the Felidae and Mustelidae* is missing. I don't dare let them leave my hands, lest they be lost. Besides, I may need them from time to time. So please don't wait for them. It's absurd not to be able to get more back copies from Vetch's publishing stocks, especially since he's still in China. Pei did not answer my letter of June. Either he hasn't received it, or (as I wrote via Hong Kong to Grootaers, a Chinese friend) it's not a good idea now for a Chinese to write to capitalist countries. (Grootaers wrote me a card from Saigon which he signed along with Kermadec. He's going to Japan. He can't get a visa to go back to China. However, the present director of the Pasteur In-

**Renowned Catholic University, Shanghai.
*The cat family and the weasel family.

stitute in Shanghai, whom I met recently, has received a reentry visa.)

In my life, there is nothing new. At the end of October, I went to Belgium for two days to give conferences at Liège and Brussels (the Provincial of southern Belgium came) and to speak at dinners. It was all too crowded and fatiguing, but interesting. I'm really quite worn out. I know that I made a good impression there, but I don't know what Rome thinks. Naturally, I did not see Charles**—not even the tip of his nose. He didn't have to come, and he probably thought it would be better if we didn't meet each other on his own ground.

Just now, I finished my auto-psychoanalytic essay "Le Coeur de la Matière" (about 60 pages) which I'm about to stencil for very private distribution. I'm not too clear about what purpose it will serve. But I'm happy that I wrote it. Now I must prepare a private conference for the Congrès de Croyants on "The Thirst for Life," considered as the fundamental biological source of cosmogenesis. Afterward, decidedly, I'm going to give a series of seminars at the Sorbonne in December–January on the "Phylogenic Structure of the Human Group," a second rewrite of *The Phenomenon of Man*, but better focused, I hope. And I plan to pass the memoir on to the *Annales de Paléontologie* without asking anything of Rome. This time it is a specifically scientific essay and I've written twice to Gorostarzu about it (true, the letters required no reply, but they provided occasions for Rome to write to me).—All this seems a bit ominous.—In an attempt to clear the air, I told Goro about my South African project. It is possible that this eventuality (my plunge back into science for a while outside Paris) may be a satisfying solution to the present tension, which is undeniable.—D'Ouince will go to Rome on November 25 to speak at the Jubilee Year symposium of the commission of bishops and religious. It's a tribute to him. But I

**Pierre Charles, Belgian Jesuit, philosopher and missiologist. Seminary classmate of Teilhard, and one-time liberal theologian, who grew extremely conservative after World War II, and often tried to induce Teilhard to moderate his views. M.L.

wonder if, under the honorific appearances, he isn't really being called to Canossa? The Roman integrists seem disappointed and irritated over the way the Encyclical "flopped" in France. The article that Roquette wrote at *Etudes* has been judged unsatisfactory, so he's preparing a second, more energetic one. Two new books by de Lubac have been removed from the bookstores. All the while the world agonizes, unable to find its way, because the Church, keeper of the flame of modern monotheism, refuses to give it the God it waits for. I grow indignant when I hear people (even Lejay!) say that all things being equal, the Encyclical is not too bad; and that it's relatively progressive when compared to the religion of the Christian masses. Don't such men see that the real question is not one of knowing whether or not the Church conserves its internal coherence, but of whether or not it can recognize that, with the miserably tepid kind of adoration it promotes, it is capable of performing its specific function—that of inflaming the earth?

No, I am not bitter. I'm as optimistic as possible. But I feel so strongly that from now on nothing will make me budge an inch from my conviction that what we now need—because the human spirit is changing—is a richer image of God. To tell the truth, glimpsing and helping to unveil this new face of God (as a prolongation of the Christian phylum) has become the single real interest and the great joy of my life.

At *Etudes* many people are not well . . .

. . . Tomorrow there is a meeting at Lejay's on the subject of the Encyclical. It really doesn't interest me too much. What really matters is not that we recognize and count faith not immediately "in the Supernatural," but in the "Ultra-Human." I am persuaded that *everything* hangs on such a faith. How many dead leaves there are even among those one would expect to be healthy!

Courage.

> And most affectionately,
> TEILHARD

69

LETTERS FROM MY FRIEND TEILHARD

Paris, December 7, 1950

Dear Friend,

... Here life continues in a fairly tense atmosphere at the ecclesiastical level. But it's a tension which in one sense only excites me. D'Ouince is in Rome at the Conference of Religious Orders, where he will make one of the principal speeches. The interesting thing would be to know what the General will tell him in private. Down in Rome they still consider France the great peril and chief culprit. Basically, according to some people who have come back from Rome, it was a report by Dhanis* on the French scholasticates after his visit of 1948 which released the avalanche. The General found it so "frightening" that he referred it to the Pope (?!). Hence the purge at Fourvière and the Encyclical. True or not true in detail, the fact remains that during the years 1930–1946, in the course of which the Parisian-Lyonnais Jesuit Group "La Pensée"** never ceased advancing our notion of Christ and Christianity, the Belgo-Romano Jesuits stood stock still —so much so that now the Belgo-Romanos honestly cannot understand the kind of Christianity that has become "ordinary" to us. Hence the panic, and (to repeat my comparison) the bombardment of the avant-garde. It's tragic, since it's fundamentally a misunderstanding. But I foresee that just as in 1930, when "La Pensée was first dispersed, the bombardés" will cling to their positions (since, by virtue of their very fidelity to the Church, they cannot leave them), and ultimately they will reemerge. For they alone are truly active and capable of communicating their thought, since they alone have "adapted" to the new world.

... We should recognize, as Jouve says, that d'Ouince is an absolute model of patience and tenacity. He moves back only

*Edouard Dhanis, Belgian ultra-conservative theologian, who made an examination of the French scholasticates in 1948. After Vatican II, he worked in ecumenicism. He died in 1978.
**Private study group of young scholastics, then at Lyon, who met in their free time to explore the writing of the more advanced thinkers in the Order. M.L.

"step by step." The articles and books of de Lubac and Brouillard, however, are withdrawn from the bookstores and the libraries of the scholasticate, the immediate effect of which action is, of course, to make the demand for them and the use of them increase. All this must not be taken too tragically. I remain convinced that "the wall is breached" and that we are the ones who have the upper hand. It's sad though that we have to learn once more that no spiritual threshold can be crossed without struggle and shock. We French too easily imagined that evolution was so obvious that it could not be denied.

Momentarily, I'm expecting to receive the stenciled copies of my new essay "Le Coeur de la Matière," an essay which I told you is a reconstruction of my interior evolution. I'll send you a copy so that you can give me your impressions. Of course, the distribution will be extremely limited. Next I will write the first draft of the five lectures (seminars) to be given at the Sorbonne. As I said, I'm going to send them to the *Annales de Paléontologie* without asking anything from anybody. What appears there cannot be criticized as "unscientific"!

More later—when d'Ouince returns.

Affectionately,
TEILHARD

1951

Teilhard with J. T. Robinson in Africa

T he two pivotal events of the next few months are Teilhard's trip to South Africa and his letter to the Father General written on October 12, 1951.

Though as the year began, his personal life was in a state of calm, the international scene was full of turbulence. War raged bitterly in Korea. Having crossed the 38th Parallel, the soldiers of the North, aided by the Chinese, reached the outskirts of Seoul and later the northern port of Hungnam. By January 1, in a second offensive they forced the United Nations troops south of River Han. On January 4, Seoul fell, and the UN retreat continued.

The dangerous developments in Asia did not surprise Teilhard. He looked at what was happening there, even with the suffering it implied, as inevitable. It was the turmoil that accompanied the awakening aspirations of the people on that continent. At the same time it gave warning of the changes that humanity and the church must undergo to understand them. Remaking oneself in this way, or "shedding an old skin" as Teilhard put it, always entailed great pain. The changes to be made to meet new challenges were not superficial, but profound. This meant that a complete rethinking of old values and institutions had to be undertaken so that spirit could be liberated. . . .

"There can be no summits without abysses," he wrote me that year.

In early 1951, Teilhard again had the opportunity to reflect publicly on the future of man. His former pupil, Professor Jean Piveteau, had asked him to give five lectures at the Sorbonne. Before an audience of nearly 80 students, he explored the problem of the "Phyletic structure of the human group."

But more personal trouble was on its way. An ex-Dominican named Denys Gorce published some articles on his ideas in Switzerland, and Rome took fright again. In an attempt to defend himself, he gave an interview to Marcel Brion of Nouvelles Littéraires and re-explained his thought. The world, he said, is in the process of construction (Cosmogenesis). The goal of cosmogenesis is man (anthropogenesis). As mankind lives and grows, it is indispensable that our idea of "humanism" change to represent it adequately. A new updated "humanism" (a "neohumanism") is therefore a necessity. As Teilhard saw it, this neohumanism must of necessity include a morality—in other words, it has to be religious.

In an address given at about this time, Julian Huxley expressed similar ideas. To Teilhard's delight, a project for studying "the scientific history of human development," making it possible for people of the highest intellectual calibre to concern themselves with this (to his mind) vital question, was begun at UNESCO.

Meanwhile, in New York Paul Fejos, director of the Wenner-Gren Foundation for Anthropological Study, also showed considerable interest in the problem. Teilhard finally succeeded in winning the backing of that organization for his African venture. Going to Africa, however briefly, was a happy solution to some of his problems in that it alleviated his financial worries and assured him that he would be able to continue his research on man. Doubtless he did entertain some fear about cutting his ties with Paris. But the tension among French Catholics regarding him had left him little choice.

By the end of January 1951, he had already booked his passage for Africa on a steamer leaving in July.

PREPARATIONS FOR THE VOYAGE

A few months before he left, however, a new sadness touched him. Lucien Cuénot, the eminent scientist, whose student I had been before I left for China, died early that year. Teilhard knew how much my study with the celebrated master of Nancy had done for me. Lucien Cuénot was a man peculiarly gifted for research and teaching. A zoologist and biologist, he also inquired into philosophical problems such as the notion of "invention"—numerous examples of which one finds among living things. Teilhard's idea that spirit manifests itself through complications of biochemical arrangements, because matter and spirit are indissolubly linked, echoed the intellectual preoccupations of Cuénot. Though he had always been tormented by metaphysical questions and ended in a scepticism bordering on agnosticism, it was reported that a Jesuit from Nancy attended at his deathbed. The grand old man closed his eyes in January 1951 after having spent his last months working on his posthumously published book Biological Evolution.

In Early February Teilhard sent the text of the lectures he had given at the Sorbonne to a publisher. The project gave him pleasure, but he was unhappy with the thought that he had nothing more to do. In reality though, he had quite a bit to occupy him, whether he liked it or not. There were new attacks against him published in the conservative France Catholique *to which he gave answer in a series which discussed those French thinkers at whom it believed "Humani Generis" was aimed. Both his superior René d'Ouince and his provincial Jacques Goussault rose to his defense.*

In this next group of letters, the reader will find, among other things, mention of the relationship between Auguste Valensin and Teilhard. It would perhaps be helpful to stop here and comment on the quality of their friendship. Cultivated, learned, a philosopher and spiritual master, Father Valensin was one of Teilhard's closest confidants. Their friendship went back to

77

their years of novitiate in Aix-en-Provence from 1900. In the first years of their priesthood, Valensin's influence on Teilhard was considerable. "I will never make a truly major decision without telling you about it," Teilhard wrote him.* Nevertheless, as time went on, the two men saw things less and less the same. Teilhard's "evolutionist adventure" was never particularly attractive to the essentially other-worldly mind of Valensin.

Though over the years they rarely saw each other, their correspondence, especially in the twenties and thirties, was extensive. Teilhard always consulted his friend when he faced a major crisis. In spring of 1951, he had "a delightful conversation with A. Valensin—one of those conversations where one says everything without reticence." But he did not draw from the exchange the benefit that he expected. Father Valensin had a "quasi-infantine religious faith" coupled with a "complete intellectual skepticism." This psychological duality offended the synthesizing mind of Teilhard. I have certainly not the right to make a value judgment on the quality of so great a personality as Valensin. Still I believe that, since Valensin's piety was nourished at another source, Teilhard's evolutionist perspective of the universe was meaningless to him. An aesthete has neither the same preoccupations nor the same vision as a scientist. Teilhard understood the study of the past as a natural complement to revelation: and he felt that just as belief in the immobility of the earth had paralyzed theology up until the day when Copernicus and Galileo proved, by the observation of phenomena, the existence of a non-geocentric universe so in our own day the discovery of evolution (i.e., organic time) had demonstrated a physical relationship between all things in creation, and destroyed forever the notion that a cosmos composed of individually cre-

---

**Lettres de Teilhard à Valensin*, published by Aubier, March 1972 (with a commentary by Henri de Lubac) are most informative. I, in my commentary in this book, have decided not to draw a parallel between that set of letters and this one. Not that it would not be instructive to do so in the future, as it would shed considerable light on Teilhard's psychology. For the moment, I wish only to add some personal impressions, however limited they may be. (P.L.)

ated beings had come into existence at one stroke. The importance to theology of this second discovery can not be overrated.

Furthermore, for Teilhard it was no longer a question of
giving moral and juridical explanations to the ultimately inexplicable mysteries of faith. The problem was one of inserting
the mystery of the Incarnation into the moving history of
humanity. When Christ bent himself to the exigencies of the human condition, he had to follow the logical consequences of that
condition to the end. A term in Teilhard's writings which often
disturbed his superiors was, therefore, "pan-Christicism." By
this word he did not mean the identification of Christ with the
world; that would be clearly heretical. But it should be considered as the union between the world as explained by science and
God, the Heart of Love.

In 1951, the renewal of the Easter Liturgy was in progress.
Père Doncoeur, a man of courage and initiative, had gathered a
circle of fervent Christians in a private house in the Paris sub-
urbs and, with the assistance of a few other priests, had thrown
over liturgical custom by consecrating a "galette"* which the
participants then broke themselves. At the time the step was au-
dacious. Today we would think nothing of it.

As revolutionary as it may have seemed then, it was an affair of small importance, and despite any psychological impact
they may have had on the participants, liturgical reforms are not
enough to answer the needs of our times. In these attempts,
Teilhard saw a diversion rather than a remedy. What he prayed
for was a change in the mentality of the teaching Church—an
enlargement of the Primacy of Christ to include the "entire universe." It was not a simple question of changing words, but of
widening concepts. It was not merely a question of changing
words or etiquette, but of remaking its official Christology. The
Church, he felt, must learn to profit from the fresh blood in-
fused by the idea of evolution, in order to give new life to Christian aspirations.

*A flat cake, thicker than a pancake.

LETTERS FROM MY FRIEND TEILHARD

The date set for the voyage to Africa came ever closer, without Teilhard's being able to face up to its inevitability. It is easy to understand why it was unimaginable to him. At two different times in recent years, Teilhard had been seriously ill. His age was weighing on him. He had passed his 70th birthday, and he no longer felt the attraction of adventure in an unknown, far-off place. The whole effort in fact, seemed beyond his strength.

Finally, however, his apprehension vanished. The voyage was decided on. He would go where he must to meet the South African paleontologists and discuss with them the geological age of the rich fossiliferous deposits found with the Australopithecines.

As he looked forward to the voyage, however, scientific preoccupations were not his major interest. Beyond the occupations of the moment, his gaze remained fixed on the future. As he saw it, a psychic explosion, a capital change which would affect humanity on the whole, was coming soon; and man must be prepared.

Teilhard wanted to find a formula—to say nothing of a morality—which would throw into relief the importance of human phenomena from both a biological and spiritual point of view. But how was one to plan a field of research for a body of learning which kept growing at every level? What interior attitude should be recommended to those whose lives were devoted to the extension of knowledge, and thus who were en route toward the summit of knowledge? How was one to understand the new field of eugenics, in which men had just begun to dabble? How was one to assimilate into this Weltanschaunng the future discovery of planets and other galaxies, where life and reflection would certainly appear?

Here one sees the essential lines of Teilhardian philosophy. The very dynamism of human Evolution consists in orientating oneself toward a quest of that greater fullness of being that can only be found in contact with Christ. It was, therefore, necessary to find the means to reach this point; and the improvement of the human species (through morally acceptable procedures) seemed to be one of the necessary conditions of this process.

The multiplicity of thinking planets—an idea which new scientific data leads us now to view as increasingly probable—called for a total reconstruction of our concept of the universe. It demanded a formal rejection of geocentricity, and an acceptance of the idea of the extension of Spirit-Matter throughout the entire universe. Given the great distances which separate the galaxies, and the limitations placed on communication with them by the barrier of the speed of light however, it seems, in my personal opinion, most unlikely that we will ever make direct contact with any intelligences from outside our solar system. Inclusion in the total universe of all the other reflective beings it may contain does, nevertheless, enrich our concept of the breadth of Christ's dominion.

In mid-June 1951, one of our colleagues, Father de Breuvery, came back from Shanghai. He had been there when the communists took over that city of merchants and bankers, and he had seen the resistance of the Chinese Catholics. Their heroism as praised by our colleague was, Teilhard said, "probably true . . . But I can't conclude that it is because of their Catholicism that the faithful Chinese are better armed to face the Marxism of Mao."

In his letters to me at that time, Teilhard spoke of de Breuvery's return as hearsay, and in passing. But at that moment, our one-time friend from China was far from leaving Teilhard's life. Teilhard would see him again, and sooner than he thought.

Paris, January 1, 1951

Dear Friend,

Here—a little late, I'm afraid—is the answer to your letter of December 19th. I only hope that the political thunderclouds now hanging over the world in this fateful year of 1951 will not burst, and set everything adrift (my own plans included!). In any case, I send warmest, most affectionate wishes for your own progress in the coming months.—Paradoxically enough, I don't feel terribly anxious when I contemplate the present tension. If my prognosis is correct, it is not only to be expected, but perhaps, under the circumstances, it is what we should be waiting for. Certainly, I have a real horror of war (which I believe to be a mode of human action that will one day simply perish by its own murderous hand). But even more, I am convinced of the absolute necessity that mankind (and more specifically, the Church) must shed its skin (or rather its old way of thinking); and perhaps, this can only happen as the result of some great shock. Mankind can no longer achieve anything important without taking stock of the (organic) movement which pulls it forward and in which man must play his part. It may be that this awareness can only be born as the result of some violent upheaval. It is to this painful conclusion that I've been forced by the attitude of Rome during the Holy Year of 1950.

Despite these stark reflections, please don't think I'm dark and bitter. On the contrary, never have I felt the power and worth of the Christique "potential" more strongly than I do right now. It is this "potential" which struggles for release in the world. These last few years, the whole "nucleus" of my interior perspective has been the search for what can be deduced by transposing into Cosmogenetic terms the traditional Vision of Reality once expressed in terms of "Cosmos."—Creation, Spirit, Evil, God (and more specifically, Original Sin), the Cross, the Resurrection, the Parousia, and Charity—all these great themes clarify and cohere in an absolutely breathtaking way, once we transpose them into Cosmogenetic terms. When I write this down (about 10 pages), I'll send it to you. Incidentally, I did send you a copy of "Le Coeur de la Matière" a week ago. You should receive it soon despite the Christmas rush.

Otherwise, there's nothing very new. Friday, I begin my course at the Sorbonne on the "Phyletic Structure of the Human Group." I'll give five lectures, once a week until I finish, and my text is already three-quarters written. I would have liked to have had a very small group of advanced students, but Piveteau, who is backing the series, tells me that it will be a class of twenty. Too bad that.—In any case, despite some horribly compromising articles about me (the last of which were published in Switzerland by an ex-Dominican named Gorce, whom I really thought I could trust!), Rome seems more easy about me at the moment. (The proof of that is d'Ouince's recent return from there in surprisingly good humor.) I'm fairly sure they're reassured because I let them know about my voyage to South Africa.

Any moment now the *Nouvelles Littéraires* is going to bring out an interview with me (d'Ouince has read and approved it) in which I clarify my thoughts as they relate to all those injurious stories circulating about me. The interview (signed by Marcel Brion) is quite well done and covers two full pages.

. . . As I see it, the Asian threat is not a real peril, since it's only the result of the pressure of great numbers. "Ideologies," not numbers, are the really dangerous things. Unless there is some drastic change, I can't conceive of a specific "Asian ideology" at this point. And without an "ideology," how can Asia "lead the world"? From now on, in my opinion, it will not be for the "possession," but for the "leadership" of the world that future wars will be fought.—I could be all wrong about this, though.

Recently I had the pleasure of meeting Julian Huxley. If you can find it, do read the discourses he gave on the occasion of the presentation of the Huxley Medal (1950), published by the Royal Anthropological Society. It is called "New Bottles for New Wine: Ideology and Scientific Knowledge," and is an appeal for the construction of an "ideology" of evolution (for "ideology" read "faith"). It's very curious, and has been strongly influenced by me, at least insofar as it talks about its most interesting point, convergence. If you get it, you can read between the lines the proposal for establishing the "Institute for Advanced Studies" to work out a "human ideology," I think I wrote about to you in an earlier letter. Huxley spent a week here trying to set up a project on "the scientific history of the development of humanity" in conjunction with UNESCO.

. . . Christmas night I dined with Dr. W.H. Wong (!) in Paris now, still unchanged under his great felt hat and overcoat, with his charming yellow smile—so sweetly and pathetically calm. He's given up his plan to go to America, and has decided to go back to Hong Kong to rejoin his father and his wife instead. He says that it is the policy of the new Chinese government to preserve everything which "works," even at the price of increasing subsidies. So the personnel and mechanism of the Geological Survey has been kept together and financed to the point of being engaged in publishing a long series of pages on the map of China. C.C. Young seems to have left the field in order to join a sort of political cabinet (!), and J.S. Lee is serving with the government in Peking. I have no special information about Pei, but the Academia Sinica is functioning again.

. . . Still no news from Fejos about Africa. I'm too sure of his friendship to doubt his interest in me. Perhaps he's traveling.

Again, happy New Year.

Affectionately,
TEILHARD

Paris, January 28, 1951

Dear Friend,

. . . Nothing particularly new right now. Next Friday, I finish my series of courses ("seminars") in the Sorbonne geology department on the "Phyletic Structure of the Human Group." As I look back on them I find that giving these lectures interested me very much. And the final version (which I have written out in the hope of doing a piece for the *Annales de Paléontologie*) is noticeably different from the essay whose publication Rome stopped six months ago. In any case, it keeps me busy!

I should tell you that I finally did get an answer from Fejos about my grant. Nothing will be decided before the foundation board meets (in March?), he says, but the situation does look favorable. I have already made a provisional reservation on the *Union Castle*, leaving for Africa July 15. . . .

. . . On the ecclesiastical side, calm still reigns. Actually, I'm doing nothing to annoy anyone. In a long interview ("A Conversation With . . .") which appeared in the *Nouvelles Littéraires* of January 11, I arranged with Marcel Brion (in a text I wrote myself and d'Ouince checked) to say that I want to make my real intellectual position public and thus clear up the false interpretations (millenialism and Hinduism) with which too many people saddle me.

I explain the heart of my position as clearly as I can: Cosmogenesis, of which anthropogenesis is the point, exists; and Anthropogenesis is still in progress—hence the need for and beginning of a *neo*humanism. All this is neither philosophy nor theology. It is the simple act of recognizing an experimentally observable movement. . . .

. . . You probably know that dear Professor Cuénot died. Naturally, the press was unanimous in its eulogy of him.

Another death which we had expected for a long time was that of the sister of Malvina Hoffman.* Despite the bitterness of separation, Malvina should feel materially liberated now.

Here at *Etudes* everything continues towards an uncertain future! I do not particularly believe that the Korean War will escalate. But the political atmosphere is terribly charged just the same.

Affectionately always,
TEILHARD

---

*Malvina Hoffman (1887–1966), American sculptor of the bronzes of racial types for the Field Museum. Lived in Paris from 1924 after which time she became acquainted with Teilhard through the Abbé Breuil. Settled in America before World War II.

LETTERS FROM MY FRIEND TEILHARD

Paris, February 15, 1951

Dear Friend,

. . . I finished my course of lectures at the Sorbonne without difficulty, and to the end I gave it with real pleasure, because I knew my audience (Pruvost, professor of geology at the Sorbonne included) was prepared for what I had to say, and did not consider me para- or extra-scientific. The text, finally written and condensed (about 40 pages) is already in the hands of Piveteau who plans to publish it in the next issue of the *Annales de Paléontologie*, between a treatise on the Lamellibranchiata of Madagascar and another on the Pliocene fossils of Auvergne. Published in such a journal, Rome cannot claim my article passes the bounds of science. It does conclude, however, on the note (for which I give solid reasons of fact) that the end of the human species must come in an "escape" out of time-space, rather than in "extinction." This makes the whole situation (particularly since I taught the course at the Sorbonne) rather piquant, don't you think?

And, suddenly, I find myself unoccupied. I'm keeping busy thinking over a short but substantial essay on "Cosmos and Cosmogenesis" (which will culminate with a definition of a "God of Cosmogenesis"), and trying to catch up on South African geology. The upcoming voyage there still seems so unreal to me! . . .

. . . Before Cuénot's death, Andrée Tétry was able to see the first 17 galleys of the Professor's book, scheduled to be published by Masson in May. It's very different from "La Jeunesse des Espèces." At the end of his life, it seems that Cuénot was not particularly close to classical Catholicism. If my understanding is correct, he seems scarcely to have believed in personal survival. Just the same, he did receive Extreme Unction (I wonder if he was conscious!). Before events like this, we must remind ourselves that "everything that rises, meets." In considering cases like this one, I am deeply struck by the size of the adjustment Christianity must make if it is to take up its conquering march again. Yes, I repeat what I have said so often before. Only a

"God of Cosmogenesis" can compel the adoration of modern man....

... Most people here at *Etudes* are down with the grippe (nothing really serious), and I've escaped so far. Last week, *France Catholique** began a series of long articles called "*Apropos the Encyclical*" (!) in which the first article was totally devoted to me! (It was written by a professor of the Institut Catholique, the Abbé Cignet, a specialist in the 17th century!) And it will be followed by two other articles (also about me) as well as pieces on several other people who will be taken to task in the rest of the series. (I wonder who—De Lubac?) The tone of the piece is sympathetic, but d'Ouince and Goussault are a little shaken. The next issue will show us whether or not a full-scale attack is planned.

And that's the news. I'm sure that I've forgotten something. But let it go for the next time.

> Affectionately as always,
> TEILHARD

Paris, March 28, 1951

Dear Friend,

... Time passes imperceptibly. I've let myself be drawn into the writing of two new essays which are being stenciled right now. One is on Cosmos and Cosmogenesis, and the other on the Ultra-Human. And when I'm writing, I always get behind on correspondence.

Honestly, though, there's nothing to report.... In most areas, everything is calm—except that we've just been reading a kind of "Super-Encyclical" direct from the Father General, which has left everybody here baffled—and unchanged. I can't see now how the professors of philosophy and theology (no mat-

---

*An extremely conservative religious newspaper.

ter how small their sense of mission) can now return to teaching in good conscience. As to the others—I imagine that they will all forget about the letter and keep on swimming just to save their skins (or should I say, their Faith).—Yesterday I had the most delightful conversation with Auguste Valensin. It was one of those exchanges in which one says everything quite openly and with a smile. But once again, I am surprised by the duality of my old friend's attitude: a quasi-infantile religious faith juxtaposed with a complete intellectual skepticism. In his place I should have given up believing long ago. A God Who is not the Energy of Cosmogenesis (since this is the fundamental thing that I believe) and a Catholicism which refuses to accept its place as the "phylum" wherein the highest kind of discovery of God can be made is meaningless to me. And I continue to believe (with considerable evidence) that my position corresponds, broadly speaking, to the only religious attitude compatible or even possible with a Universe, which neither the theologians, nor even de Lubac and Valensin, seem even to have glimpsed.

Through a series of happy chances these last few weeks, I've come in contact with several interesting thinkers, each one very different from the other—an experience which has helped me to get a better perspective on the world of modern thought, and to fix my own outlook better. My new friends range from Julian Huxley, with his rather boyish human faith, to Hyppolite (the charming philosophy professor from the Sorbonne) dreaming his metaphysic in which the real and the historic dissolve into a childlike intellectual "sufficiency" (as though Reason alone could bend Cosmogenesis to to its taste and caprices!) to "Sammy," a Columbia professor of mathematics (he teaches something called "topological algebra") who is now giving a course at the Sorbonne—He's a kind of young Einstein with a smiling face who absolutely devastated me with happiness by declaring publicly and quite simply that for him the only attraction of research was the possibility it offered to create something that would not die. I think I have a better grasp now of my situation.—For his part, Huxley continues to press his project of having a "brain trust" to research a "human ideology." But since I find the idea too diffuse and imprecise, I've submitted a simpler and better focused counter-project—the idea of having a sort of embryonic institute like the one at Princeton—a research institute for the study of human self-evolution. (I've made an outline for a program which I rather like.)

All this keeps me interested and involved. When I can, I continue to visit the same circle of friends. . . .

At *Etudes* all goes normally. Among ourselves, some of us were quite amused over the liturgical revolution of Holy Saturday (which some people see as a religious "event" (!). It's enough to make you bang your head against a wall! At Troussure, under the direction of some of our Fathers, they consecrated and broke a kind of cake over a cup of unconsecrated wine—just as people used to do in the fourth century, if you please!—I repeat, if I had not had the grace to see the "ever-greater Christ" as a vital condition of "ultra-hominization," I would get out of all this, even at the risk of having to beg in the streets. But I can no longer turn away from what I see. And nothing, I believe, will make me change my mind—Oh, how much we need reform—a reform not just of manners, but in our very conception of God Himself!

Again, don't think me bitter or disappointed. I am in just as good spirits as ever. But I'm also just as outspoken. *Veritas liberavit vos.*

I suppose there are innumerable little things I've forgotten to tell you. But they will wait for another time.

> With much affection,
> TEILHARD

> Paris, May 9, 1951

Dear Friend,

. . . The days are passing, and they carry me, almost without realizing it, towards a departure for Africa which still seems unreal. Happily, Rhoda is here to steer me efficiently through the preparations and formalities of travel. It is more and more evident to me that this plunge back into geology is a gesture I must make. But the gesture demands such an effort!—Well, Godspeed. . . .

. . . Recently again (I don't think I told you) I had a little trouble with Rome . . .

As I wrote to Goussault, Rome must be made to understand that there is no provocation and no rebellion in my attitude (or in that of others). It is just the uncontrollable resistance of people who struggle so as not to suffocate.

In the religious atmosphere now imposed on us, we can adore no longer. More precisely, a God and Christ of Cosmogenesis must be substituted for the God and Christ of the Cosmos which churchmen in high places continue to force on us—otherwise, all that's left is suffocation. I've written a few pages on this subject after having talked about it at Easter. . . .

Without any bitterness and with growing optimism, I see (or think I do) the "new" God rise more and more gloriously on the horizon. I can truly say that this is the deepest joy I have ever known in my life. *Nunc dimittis*. How sad it is that this vision places me in apparent conflict with the magisterium! Let us hope that I die before any real break occurs. Such an event would do more harm than good to the cause I so believe in.

Otherwise, there's not much news. At the end of May, the "Catholic Intellectuals" will hold their study week, this time on "Human Hope and Christian Hope." But except for André George and (?) Leprince-Ringuet, none of the speakers has the slightest idea of what this beautiful subject means. For all the underhumanized (Gabriel Marcel, Mauriac (!!!)), adoration is an act of escape, rather than of ultra-evolution! And not a single one of the speakers really *believes* in "human hope" itself!—At *Etudes* we are managing to stay afloat. Gorostarzu is back in France right now, but he still hasn't turned up here. It may be that he feels he'll be received politely, but a little coolly. Lejay has all sorts of meetings planned starting in June. In September,

St. Seine goes to the Congo to examine some marine strata (Jurassic?). I ran into Tétry at the Institute two weeks ago and found her very busy with Cuénot's book, which will be published by Masson at the end of May. And speaking of Masson, I'm correcting the first proofs of my treatise on "The Phyletic Structure of the Human Group" which is to appear in the next edition of the *Annales de Paléontologie.*—All this brings back memories of my first publication with Boule.*

And so you have the story of the pathetic progress of our little interests in a world where everything could explode tomorrow. Still, I am optimistic because I think I can see the process that operates at the heart of things. But what will the face of our earthly world be like in 50 years?

Affectionately always—
As ever,
TEILHARD

Paris, June 19, 1951

Dear Friend,

. . . I'm just about to leave now—may it please God. My passage to London is booked for July 5th; I will leave Southampton on the 12th; I will meet Barbour in London, and he will join me by plane at Johannesburg. . . .

Everything is going providentially well. It seems that I will be able to render a small service to the South Africans by helping them (in the capacity of adviser) to set up a plan for research (choice of fissures to work, etc.) which I will transmit to New York this fall. In one stroke then, the whole face of my voyage is

*Marcellin Boule, professor at the French National Museum of Natural History in Paris (1902–1936), and Teilhard's first mentor in paleontology in France.

transformed: collaboration and service instead of a simple quasi-touristic visit. . . .

. . . Fundamentally, however, my internal and external activity is still concentrated around the problem of disclosing—under undeniable signs, and in as scientific terms as possible—the significance of the human phenomenon, perceived as an effect of the convergence-through-arrangement of the Universe upon itself. Not an action that is slowing down (as people say—particularly in America) but one which is in full acceleration—(rather like the spatial expansion of the universe, described by astrophysics). Here, I feel, lies the capital phenomenon that must be explored, all the way from physics through its articulation in the realms of biology and spirituality. And with the help of Fejos this autumn in New York, I have considerable hope that I'll be assisting at the birth of an organization especially constructed and equipped to examine and affirm the reality of this phenomenon (a sort of little Palomar on another level). By a happy coincidence, Fejos himself is going to visit Paris next week. I wonder if this will not serve to prolong my stay in New York in November. Who knows whether it will not be there in America that we two will meet again?—But all this is so vague. I cannot even pin it down in my imagination. It could as easily be that I'll be back in Paris earlier than I plan right now.

I was very interested to hear about the convention in Atlantic City that you wrote of. It is healthy and inevitable that scientists are examining man as a kind of super-molecule. But at the same time, we must recognize that this new ever-accelerating research demands—no matter what the price—that we dare to sketch the lines of the new ethic (and theology) to energize and control without hindering it. Christification of Research, Christification of Eugenics, and Christification of our thinking about the multiplicity of our thinking about inhabited planets—these are the three vital subjects which religion should begin to examine now, since they represent the three areas on which man will have to take a stand in the next hundred years.

At *Etudes* and here in Paris there's no news. Cuénot's book

Biological Evolution (which is signed: "with the collaboration of A. Tétry") was published at the end of May by Masson. It has an excellent preface, but its ultimate conclusion is a bit vague: an appeal to pantheism, which to my mind, at least, does not show clearly enough that the universe converges. For Cuénot, at the end, Life seems to have remained something in the process of dispersion, in which man does not occupy a pivotal role nor one directed toward escape from time-space. In this book Cuénot accepts, and places in exergue before a chapter, Vandal's unhappy conclusion that Man has reached a "dead end." Too bad. Otherwise the book is a magnificent testament, worthy of a life of splendid work.

De Breuvery is just back from Hong Kong, and he lunched here today. I haven't seen him yet, so I don't know exactly what his plans are now. It seems that in a public conversation some days ago, he made a great show of his admiration for the heroic Chinese Catholics. That they are heroic is probably true. But I cannot conclude that it is because of their Catholicism that they are better armed to face the Marxism of Mao.

So many things that I meant to put into this letter which I've forgotten due to three interruptions! Now it's the 21st rather than the 19th, when I started.

I'd better stop and mail this. I'll keep you up to date as things develop.

Courage.

> Affectionately,
> TEILHARD

SOUTH AFRICA

The preparations for his trip to London and Johannesburg left Teilhard little time to write; and it was two months before I heard from him again. By that time, he had left Paris for an in-

definite length of time, and the arrangement was that at the end of his African visit, he should go to New York for a while.

When a letter dated August 15 reached me in Paris from Johannesburg, Teilhard had been in Africa three weeks. He was well pleased with his trip. In his mind, a vague nostalgia for the "imperturbably blue sky" of Peking mixed now with excitement over the flamboyant and prosperous African landscapes around him. But even more than the scenery and curiosities, he was heartened by the thought that he was doing something useful. Though the Australopithecine sites had been open for some time, because their Upper Tertiary deposits were often difficult to make out, it was a delicate matter to arrive at a good analysis of the stratigraphy. This was the work that Teilhard had come to Africa to do.

As always, the field work was a tonic for him. It put him in better spirits than he had been in for years. Unfortunately, the amelioration in his suffering was short-lived. Too soon his nervous crises came again, bringing with them all the old familiar moral and physical suffering. Only his strength of character, his strong will, and above all, his admirable resignation to his trials helped him to mask his pain and hide it from all but those who knew him intimately.

As always when he traveled, Teilhard reserved some time to write his essays. Even on the voyage out from Southampton to Cape Town, he composed a paper called "The Convergence of the Universe," which he planned to distribute in America when he arrived there in late October via Buenos Aires. Once he was in Africa, the peace of his surroundings and his involvement with his task strengthened the vision that the paper outlined. It was the "Ever Greater Christ" he wrote of—that Christ Who was neither myth nor illusion, the Redeemer of the Universe, the Lord of St. John and St. Paul. In Teilhard's mind, the Redemption extends from man to all that exists. And Christ's redemptive dominion, therefore, includes the whole of Creation.

In this vision, he only echoes St. Paul in his description of Christ to the Colossians: "The First-born of all creation, by

Whom, in Whom and for Whom all was made . . . In Whom are hidden the treasures of wisdom and of knowledge."

On September 7, Teilhard wrote me his second letter from Africa. At the moment, all still seemed to be going well. In that far-off continent, he once more breathed the exotic atmosphere of the unfamiliar that he missed since China. At Makapan he found a Lower Paleolithic strata comparable to that at Choukou-tien, the place in the Peking hills where the cranium of the Sin-anthropus was found over twenty years earlier. The comparison between the two digs is even more striking when he described the place as one in which there were traces of humanity in the process of formation.

When he was in Africa, Teilhard received a letter from An-dré Ravier, his newly-appointed major superior at Lyon, advis-ing him of his position vis-à-vis his superiors in Europe, and suggesting that he prolong his stay in America. He also suggest-ed that Teilhard write a note to Father Janssens, the General of the Order, to communicate to him his state of soul, and to ex-plain his plans for the future.

I have cited this letter extensively in an earlier book but I will include it here because I feel it is crucial to understanding Teilhard's state of mind at this time. Although he composed it on October 10, 1951, on the way back down to Cape Town, Teil-hard was extremely hesitant about mailing it. Before doing so, he sent it to Father Ravier for his approval. Anyone who doubts Teilhard's absolute fidelity should read it with attention.

In late September Teilhard sailed from the port of Durban, in northern South Africa, down the coast to Cape Town, where bad weather held him in port for several weeks. The delay gave him time to tour the surrounding countryside. It also allowed him the opportunity to write to his old and sympathetic friend, Father John LaFarge, in America advising him of his plans to stay on in New York and asking his help in finding lodgings

with the Jesuits when he arrived there. On October 15, he final-
ly sailed from Cape Town.

In the same letter in which he wrote me about his note to
LaFarge, Teilhard made an allusion to our one-time Peking publisher, Henri Vetch. The remark, though ironic, is not without
humor. During the Japanese occupation when we were working
together at the Institute of Geobiology, Vetch was one of our
closest friends. An expansive man, full of curiosity, with a great
taste for conversation, he shared a compartment with a Japanese
civilian one day on the train that went from Peking to Tientsin.
In a rather cheerful mood he chatted on and on. Finally, unable
to bear the interminable noise any longer, his companion ad-
monished him to silence. Since the Japanese knew only a few
words of English, however, he could only shake his head and
murmur, "Talk, talk, talk. Too much!" Vetch was much amused
by the incident and returned to Peking to repeat the story. Almost a decade later, however, his garrulousness led him into
much more serious problems. At the moment when Teilhard
mentioned him in this letter, Vetch was in prison under Chinese communist guard.

Teilhard reached Buenos Aires in early November 1951. "It
gives one a kind of shock," he wrote me, "to find remains of a
Permian glacier here, and Devonian sandstone similar to that
which I just left at Durban on the Cape. (A point for Wegener!)"
This remark refers to the proponent of the theory of continental
drift which was still in considerable dispute at the time. Since
then, however, the work of modern scientists has fairly well established that Wegener was correct.

Besides the geological similarities between the South African and the South American coasts, the Buenos Aires visit
touched my friend in an even more sensitive spot. As he examined ancient Indian artifacts in a museum in that city, he felt
that he was seeing the endpoint of the great human migration
that had begun in Africa, crossed Asia and followed down the
length of the Americas. The long reach of that movement,

whose first signs he had just finished examining in Africa, was brought home powerfully to him. It led him to compose his essay "On the Prolongation of the Mechanism of Evolution in Man"—a piece he wrote with even greater pleasure in that it had been requested from him for an album Julian Huxley was preparing.

Langham Hotel, Johannesburg
August 15, 1951

Dear Friend,

. . . For three weeks now, I have been in Africa, where I feel perfectly at ease, physically and morally. It's spring here—a real Peking spring, but without the sandstorms. The nights are cool (we're at an altitude of nearly 2,000 meters). The sky is imperturbably blue, with pink fruit trees blossoming in the gardens.—Jo'burg is a kind of Detroit of skyscrapers lying between areas of white slag heaps (the dumping ground from the gold fields) in the south, and a residential area of villas shaded with eucalyptus trees and mimosa in the north. There's still a kind of pioneer flavor to the place—not at all disagreeable either. Immediately on leaving Johannesburg, one falls upon a great stretch of "veldt" to the south very like the steppes of China. In the same way, the moment one leaves Pretoria, one lands right in the middle of the African bush.

But all this is just surface detail. More important to me than these exotic pictures is the feeling I have that, at last, I'm doing something really interesting. I've already gone once to the Australopithecine sites (they're quite near here), and last week I went on to the famous grottoes of Makapan (some 300 km. to the north). I'm beginning to understand the situation and am developing ideas and projects to submit to the Wenner-Gren Foundation (formerly the Viking Fund).—And incidentally, under the gentle excitement of travel and of fieldwork, it seems to me that my "fundamental vision" clarifies and deepens. Between Southampton and Cape Town I wrote a manifesto-program ("The Convergence of the Universe") which Rhoda is helping me to translate. It's a text I can produce and distribute in November when I reach America. In other words, I'm telling you that (physically) I am quite well—distinctly better than I was three years ago. For example, I'm waking up these mornings happy and clearheaded again, without anxiety—and I'm sure it is to Rhoda's management that I owe it. Without her I would not even have been able to leave Paris. I know that all too well.

Circumstances then, you understand, have placed me in a kind of life and world apart quite far from the conventional. I still feel that the Church is phyletically essential to the achievement of "the Human." But at the same time, it has become clear to me that only two things are really present in my life: a "Super-Christ" and myself. I really think that because of this central fact (because it truly *is* a question of "the Ultra-Christ"), I can look forward to closing my eyes in the end without there having been any kind of break. I pray the same for you.

I'll write you again in a little while. I plan to stay here until the end of October. I will arrive in New York (via Buenos Aires) near Thanksgiving Day.

Affectionately,
TEILHARD

Langham Hotel, Johannesburg
September 7, 1951

Dear Friend,

. . . Life continues to be interesting, under an imperturbable Peking sky. In all the gardens, under the dry sunshine (we did have one shower all the same) the fruit trees are in bloom just as they used to be in the Western Hills in March. This country is decidedly most pleasant. . . .

I think I wrote my last letter to you before I made my end-of-August trip to Kimberley (you know, the diamond city). It was a less picturesque excursion than the one to Makapan, but also very interesting. In the old gravel of the Vaal, constantly sifted by the diamond hunters, relics of the Lower Paleolithic are amazingly plentiful. It's an astonishingly smooth area (in fact, what is uncovered is the old continental surface worn away by the carboniferous moraines). It is green, as far as the eye can see, with tall grass and thorn trees where one is surprised (and regretful) not to see giraffes and rhinos moving anymore.—To finish our tour, we went to see the quarries of Taung, where in 1925 the first Australopithecus was found. A real Choukoutien, on the border of the Kalahari!—I now have almost finished making my inspection of all the essential places. I have in mind the principal elements of information I may need; and I still have six or seven weeks to put it all down in a proper report for the Wenner-Gren Foundation.

To sum up, I have learned a great deal here about the problem of human origins (even though I still haven't seen Kenya!). At the same time though (as much through reaction to the pre-Cambrian as to the Pleistocene) I leave here doubly convinced that the study of the Past is vain, if it does not end by placing us on the track of the movements (or process) which is now prolonged in us and around us, and which we must simultaneously seize and control.

From this period of isolation and contact with the changeable, I will emerge, I know, even more irrevocably committed to affirm and preach the physical, biologic reality of life's irresistible movement toward growing reflectivity. This movement is every bit as inflexible as the drive in the heart of atoms or in the galaxies. (I'm preparing a new essay—still the same old song—on "The Reflection of Energy," or rather, "The Conservation and Degradation of Energy. Remarks in the Margin of Orthodox Belief.")

I do not know where all this is going to lead me. Fundamentally I have no serious worry. The "Ultra-Christ" in no way contradicts Christ as we've always known Him. And one thing I see clearly. Nothing, absolutely nothing (except of course sickness or death), can make me leave off from exploring this concept to the end.

Good luck and warmest wishes,
TEILHARD

Mount Nelson Hotel, Cape Town
October 8, 1951

Dear Friend,

. . . As you see, I finally left (a bit regretfully) the great horizon and the magnificent sun of the Transvaal. I have left it only to find just as magnificent a springtime here (at least as far as the vegetation and the flowers are concerned.) Climatically, things are more uncertain. Exquisitely fine days are suddenly interrupted by brusque storms from the south which cover the famous "table," rising straight up just outside my window, with clouds. We came here via Durban, then the coast, by steamer—a voyage, made longer and more annoying by the constant loading and unloading of cargo, and by a bout of bad weather. Three entire days under a rainstorm at Port Elizabeth!—Just the same, I don't at all regret the difficulty. It was the price I paid for having been able to see many geologically interesting things on the edge of the continent, to say nothing of the Crossopterygian* (Lattimeria) fish caught at East London in 1937, which was shown to me by [its discoverer] Miss Lattimer herself. It was really an extraordinary spectacle—an enormous ganoid more than 2 meters long, with lobed fins!

Our ship for Buenos Aires is due here on the 15th. While I wait, I'm making some excursions. Yesterday, under a magnificent sky, I saw the countryside brilliant with flowers, a carpet of

*Crossopterygii: a fish group that may have shared a common ancestor with land vertebrates.

arums, anemones and multi-colored wild flowers, and then the heather so intensely red that it wearied the eye to look at it. The day after tomorrow (time permitting) we will go to see a new dig (Old Paleolithic with some fossils) which might deserve some backing from the Wenner-Gren.—To sum up, scientifically speaking, I have made a tour of everything I can. And I leave here satisfied. I've already sent New York a preliminary report.

Before leaving the Cape, a kind but "prudent" letter to Father Janssens—to reassure him as much as possible about my faith and my obedience, and at the same time to suggest to him provisionally that it would doubtless be advantageous that I prolong my stay in New York, where I know that Fejos will find some scientific occupation for me. When they read all this in Rome, they will be sure that I won't be doing any damage in France for a while. I only hope that the American Fathers will not take umbrage at my presence. In any case, I plan to write to LaFarge who I know will vouch for me to the American Assistant. I met the Assistant in Rome three years ago, and I don't really feel I can depend on his good feeling.

It seems an eternity since I've heard from Jouve! I hope he's well. I wrote to him about a week ago.

Between October 25 and November 10 you can reach me c/o American Express, Avenida Cordoba 854, Buenos Aires. After November 20 write me at AMERICA House, New York.

Affectionately,
TEILHARD

P.S.
Poor Vetch. He had to go and "talk, talk, talk" again. (Now what about our publications!?)

LETTERS FROM MY FRIEND TEILHARD

Buenos Aires, November 8, 1951

Dear Friend,

Yesterday I wrote to Jouve to tell him about my trip. As I explained to him, stopping in Argentina immediately after I left South Africa was very useful to me in that it brought home to me in a most vivid way (both from a geological and an anthropological point of view) the analogies and contrasts between the two continents. It is a real shock to rediscover here the results of a Permian glaciary period and some Devonian sandstone very like that which we just left at Durban and the Cape. (One point for Wegener!*) As to the study of man, that's another shock. Just after having left the hearth of "explosion" of the Paleolithic industry in Africa, I've come upon relics of the human wave at the end of its journey—after having crossed Asia and come down the length of the Americas—far in South America on the other side of the world! Unhappily, I was only able to sense this through collections and museums. But on that score, I was lucky—due to the presence here of a good, well-known German prehistorian (Dr. Oswald Menghen, who retired to Buenos Aires after the war) who is in the process of completely redoing what has been collected especially in Patagonia. At his museum, I saw a great many things which most people, outside of this country, know nothing about.—Above all, it's interesting as a contrast to see here the closure to the curve of the first "planetary" human expansion. But it's equally interesting in terms of any attempt to measure and describe the general movements of the "human phenomenon."

As to more superficial impressions (as I told Jouve) Buenos Aires is an immense Marseille, or an immense "Concession," all of whose exoticism (except for the strange fish of the Rio de la Plata in its waters) has apparently disappeared. Tomorrow I shall leave here without having seen a single blade of grass of the Argentine countryside proper. Were I to try to see it, I'd have to make an excursion of two or three days with an auto and somebody younger than I am.—Our next stop will be Rio de Janeiro, Trinidad and finally New York.

En route, I want to write some pages for a book of Julian Huxley's ("Reflections on the Prolongation of the Mechanism of Evolution in Man")—an article Huxley himself asked for.—I consider such a paper in the scientific domain and naturally will say nothing about it to anyone.—Finally, I delayed sending my letter to the Father General, but I did send a copy with some marginal notes to Father Ravier who will tell me if I risk making any trouble by sending it.

In my text, in as "filial" a tone as possible, I explain the heart of my position, why I absolutely can not change (it would be a physical impossibility), how such a position only binds me more closely to the Church of God, precisely how I now propose to explore my vision as a work of purely personal reflection with no thought of public dissemination, and what research of a purely scientific order (scientific in my definition—but that's the whole question, isn't it?) I intend to do. I conclude the letter by presenting in a rather vague way the idea of my prolonging my stay in America, as the best means of giving the storm around me time to calm down.

The only sure thing in all this is that (as long as anything remains of my health or my head) nothing can stop me from crying that "The Earth Turns!*—In other words, that humanity converges on itself. The more I think about it, the more convinced I am that the very consciousness of this movement of physical-biological-mental convergence irresistibly entails a recasting, or more exactly a total rebirth, of mystical theology and Faith on every level. If I ever reach the point of making understood the fact that evolution's nature is convergent, then everything else will be transformed. One good blow on this precise

---

*"E pur si muove"—traditionally the dying words of Galileo, and one of Teilhard's favorite references.

103

point, and everything else will splinter (or detonate, as you will).

In deep affection,
TEILHARD

P.S.

I'm adding a word for Grassé to this letter. I no longer know the number of the institute on the Boulevard Raspail. Please send it to him.

Even though the letter of Father Teilhard to Father Janssens, the General of the Order, has already been reproduced many times, it seems opportune to us to place it in this correspondence. The original, which I have before my eyes, bears some corrections by hand inscribed on the margin, which were all taken into account at the time of its first publication. The letter sums up Teilhard's intellectual and spiritual position. The humility and docility of this religious, vowed simultaneously to "remain a child of obedience" and to persevere in his research "under pain of catastrophe and infidelity to [his] most cherished vocation," is remarkable and touching.

Cape Town, October 12, 1951

V.R.F.Janssens
Rome

Very Reverend Father,
P.C.

At the moment when I am leaving Africa (that is, after two months of work and of calm in the field), I have the feeling that the time has come to send you some words to let you know what I am thinking and what I am feeling—all this, without forget-

ting that you are "The General," but at the same time (as in our
too-short conversation three years ago) in the spirit of filial
openness which is one of the most precious treasures of the Order.

1. First of all, I think you must resign yourself to accepting
me just as I am, even with the congenital quality (or weakness)
because of which, from my earliest childhood, my spiritual life
has always been completely dominated by a sort of profound
"feeling" for the organic reality of the world. It is a feeling that
at first was fairly vague in my mind and heart, but a feeling that
over the years grew to be a precise and overwhelming sense of
the general convergence of the universe upon itself—a convergence that coincides and culminates at its summit in Him *in quo
omnia constant*—He whom the Company taught me to love.

In my awareness of this synthesis of all things *in Jesu Christo*,
I have found an extraordinary and inexhaustible source of clarity and interior strength and an atmosphere outside of which it
has become physically impossible for me to breathe, to adore,
and to *believe*. And the attitude which over thirty years might
have been taken to be stubbornness or impertinence, is due simply to my powerlessness to keep my wonder before this fact
from shining outward. This is the basic psychological situation
from which everything I do and am derives. It is a trait that I
can no more change than I can change my age or the color of my
eyes.

2. With this said, and to reassure you about my interior position, I feel it necessary to insist on the fact (whether or not it
can be generalized of individuals other than myself) that the interior attitude which I have just described has, for its direct effect, my ever stronger commitment to three convictions which
form the marrow of Christianity.

These are: the unique value of Man in the path of the rise of
Life; the axial position of Catholicism in the convergent bundle
of human activities; and, at last, the essential consummating
function assumed by the Risen Christ at the center and summit
of creation. These three elements have put down and continue

to put down such deep roots throughout the system of my intellectual and religious vision, that from now on it would be impossible for me to tear them up without destroying everything.

In truth, and by the very virtue of all the structure of my thought, I feel myself today more irredeemably bound to the hierarchical Church and to the Christ of the Gospels than I have ever been at any moment in my life. Never has Christ seemed more real, more personal, or more immense to me.

How then can I believe that the direction in which I am engaged is wrong?

3. Finally, I fully recognize that Rome may have its reasons for believing that in its present form my vision of Christianity is premature or incomplete, and that as a consequence, it cannot presently be diffused without creating problems.

It is on this important point of exterior fidelity and docility that I wish particularly to assure you (and this is the essential point of this letter) that, despite certain appearances, I am determined to remain "a child of obedience."

Evidently (under the pain of an interior catastrophe and infidelity to my most cherished vocation) I cannot leave off exploring this path privately. But (and this has been the case for some months) I am no longer occupied with the propagation of my ideas, only with deepening them within myself. This attitude is greatly facilitated for me by the fact that I am now engaged in direct scientific work.

I have reason to hope that my absence from Europe will simply cause the agitation about me, which has disturbed you recently, to subside. In this matter, Providence seems to hold out a hand. The Wenner-Gren Foundation in New York (formerly the Viking Fund), which sent me here (it is the same Foundation, incidentally, which, after the war, set up Fr. Schmidt's "Anthropus" project) has already asked me to prolong my stay in America as long as possible in order to straighten out and enlarge upon the results of my field work. This will give me time, and will direct me toward a wholly scientific end to my career, and my existence.

Let me repeat to you that I write these lines to be a simple opening of conscience. I expect no answer from you. I only hope that you will see in them how fully you can count on me to work toward the Kingdom of God, which is all that fills my mind, and which leads me on by way of Science.

Very respectfully yours in Christo Filius,
P. TEILHARD DE CHARDIN

AT THE WENNER-GREN FOUNDATION IN NEW YORK

In the next selection of letters, we find Teilhard "solidly anchored at the Wenner-Gren Foundation." His projects were delineated: "the organization of world research concerning human origins" and the completion of the "forces of speciation in contemporary humanity."

Unexpected encouragement came to him from Rome. The Father-General answered his Cape Town letter and approved his stay with the foundation.

Thus, it was with a free heart that he took up his work in New York. He happily visited his friends at the Museum of Natural History, where he barely missed seeing George Simpson, the neo-Darwinian biologist who is responsible for many important works on evolution quite opposed to the Teilhardian vision. The situation vis-à-vis American churchmen was less reassuring. But Teilhard hoped that all would turn out for the best.

News of the failing health of Raymond Jouve, the administrator of Etudes and Teilhard's devoted friend, left him desolate. "I'm going to write to him soon—To come to the point of penetrating, seeing, and loving the warm presence of God amid all the implacable, blind and icy determinisms of the world—what a problem! And what a triumph!"

LETTERS FROM MY FRIEND TEILHARD

Wenner-Gren Foundation
14 East 71st Street, New York 21, N.Y.
December 10, 1951

Dear Friend,

... As far as things go here, you know the situation. If Rome does not "have a change of heart" and if our American Fathers are not too "upset" about me, it seems that I am now solidly anchored in the Wenner-Gren Foundation, where Fejos gave me a touching welcome. I see my work here on three levels (going from the outside inward):

—collaboration with the organization's research in the area of human origins (my "grant" will be taken care of as a research associate for paleoanthropology);

—an effort to investigate scientifically the problem of the prolongation (under what form, I wonder?) of the biological forces of evolution and of speciation in contemporary humanity;

—lastly (for myself alone) a continuation of my effort to synthesize the *En Haut* and the *En Avant* into a single religious thought (a Christology), adjusted to the new size of the universe.

As to my feeling my way on the middle plane, Fejos seems entirely conquered by me; and he will open up desirable contacts with the best thinkers in this country and elsewhere. I will begin with private or semiprivate conversations. I will take one further step this summer when the foundation holds an important symposium on anthropology (65 participants invited from everywhere at the Wenner-Gren's expense). It takes place here in June, with the stated purpose of establishing an account of the results attained and the problems posed by anthropology.— Had I known about this earlier I would have done what I could to have Grassé from France invited: his knowledge of biology would have enlivened the symposium on human materials a hundred times better than the osteological reports of certain other participants.

Naturally, between Rome and our American Fathers, I'm still treading a little on thin ice. But I am confident the situation will stabilize. The other evening I dined at America House where the new team (LaFarge and Gardiner alone represent the old guard) received me most cordially and made an excellent impression on me. I still haven't seen my friends from Fordham (Ewing, who has dug at Beirut, and some others probably). . . .

Visited Malvina in her studio. She seems much recovered from the death of her sister and from her brief and painful sciatica of this summer, just as luminous as ever, imperturbably open and active. The plan for the mausoleum commemorating the Americans who fell at Epinal is still in force (*mirabile dictu!*). She continues to work, and will go to France next May. I made my first visit to the Natural History Museum, where I spent most of my time with Colbert. Simpson is on a year's vacation in his new house in New Mexico, writing two books (the more important one, I think, is on the general principles of biology). I still haven't run into Gregory.

And that's about it for the moment. Sometimes I have a vague sense of homesickness in being so cut off from Paris.— But there are compensations. And the feeling will pass. The important thing is that I may be able to do something good here.

I'm quite distressed, as I told you in the beginning, at the state of Jouve's health, which, alas, stems from a deep organic cause. Please assure him of my warm affection. I'm going to write to him—To reach the point of penetrating, seeing, and loving the warm presence of God amid all the implacable blind and icy determinisms of the world—what a problem! And what a triumph! . . .

> Always in deep affection,
> As ever,
> TEILHARD

1952

Teilhard at Glacier Lake, Montana

Nineteen fifty-two was the year when Teilhard's correspondence with me was most regular and abundant. It accounts for nineteen letters, written between January 13 and December 24. The main event of this period was Teilhard's definitive installation in America. As a staff member of the Wenner-Gren Foundation, he made his home in New York City. From then on, the question of returning to France and taking up any further work there no longer existed.

Thus it was from the other side of the Atlantic that my friend pursued his scientific work and wrote the final pages of his philosophic and religious works.

We must go back a little now, to properly understand the details and the ideas which form the framework for this correspondence. At this time, Teilhard was, once more, practically in exile. But in none of his letters did he allude to his pain. His mind and heart retained their old vivacity.

On January 13, 1952, he wrote me that he had completed a Note for the Academy of Sciences on his African adventures. He wanted to arrange for his colleagues at the Institute to share his observations on the Australopithecines. His thoughts on the matter were as follows:

LETTERS FROM MY FRIEND TEILHARD

"The group there is in a state of rapid evolution. Their very variety allows us to affirm that, judging by the character of their dentition, the Australopithecines—though quite far from all known anthropomorphs—parallel the human type of dentition in an astonishing way. They form a separate group situated between the anthropomorphs and the true hominians."

From these considerations, he drew the following conclusions:

By virtue of their intercalary type, a relationship between the anthropomorphs and the hominians exists; their presence provides a further argument in favor of the thesis of the African origin of the human group; lastly, "the idea that the human group initially possessed and still virtually possesses the branching structure" of the great phylums, was confirmed. Later research has not much modified these views. Essentially, Teilhard was not mistaken.

In further comment on the subject of man, Teilhard often emphasized his wish to see the study of the human phenomenon moved from the domain of Letters to that of Science. Apropos this matter, he had a "long and charming letter" from Filmer S.C. Northrop, professor of the philosophy of law at Yale University. But their respective positions were completely opposed. While Teilhard considered "the deep-seated identification between natural and cultural evolution" as a fundamental fact of experience, to Northrop, it remained a question of words. In the June symposium, therefore, Teilhard saw the opportunity of engaging in a battle of ideas and defending his point of view. Furthermore, he dreamed of another symposium on Man to be held later—one which would bring together not only anthropologists, but biologists, chemists and nuclear physicists.

When he met Margaret Mead, he thought perhaps they understood each other. At about that time he also found an echo of his thought in a book called Time's Arrow and Evolution *written by Princeton Professor H.F. Blum, which sought to trace the origin of life and insisted on the complexity of its chemical components. Teilhard recommended the book to me as one which followed his own line of thought.*

At the moment, he was also busy composing a report to present at the June symposium replacing Le Gros Clark, who was then lecturing in Australia. Written in English, the paper was a history of the discovery of Fossil Man over the last century. It also reflected the ideas of the author on the place of man in nature.

When the symposium took place at last, Teilhard made contact with John Stuart, director of the Princeton Observatory, and Roger Williams, director of an Institute of Biochemistry in Austin, Texas. He also lectured on the Australopithecines at both the New York Academy of Sciences and the Wenner-Gren Foundation. Occasional encounters with friends such as Malvina Hoffman, Lucile Swan, and Tillie Hoffman, a one-time member of the staff of the American Embassy in Peking, somewhat brightened his daily routine.

He often thought of Paris and his old friends, Pierre de St. Seine, Jean Piveteau and Pierre-Paul Grassé, who occupied the chair of evolution of organized beings at the Sorbonne. And when he heard of the death of our old colleague, Emile Licent, he was moved to comment: "A real loss, despite everything."

ORTHOGENESIS

Teilhard's letter of March 16 is particularly interesting because it exposes his thought on two points of theoretical biology. It was an old problem that he discussed. As long ago as April 1947, an international conference had been held in Paris to compare the paleontologists' and geneticists' points of view on transformist theories. At that time, the questions of Orthogenesis and of Finality were discussed without any unanimous conclusion being reached.

"Orthogenesis" is a term which was first utilized in 1893 by a now forgotten man, the biologist Wilhelm Haacke. Later, Gustav Eimer gave it a definition as "that general law according to which evolutionary development takes place in a noticeable direction, above all in specialized groups."

Many biologists have been uncomfortable with this term,

which according to George Simpson, includes "an element of mysticism," and as such is unacceptable to the scientific domain. Other scientists (Lucien Cuénot, for one) believed that "the variations of a given series seem to be channelled in a certain direction, as if oriented toward some kind of goal."

In his letter of March 16, 1952, Teilhard recognized that the interpretation of biologists is delicate on this point "because they perceive a philosophical intrusion there (Finality . . . directed by creative idea)." But for him, this is a vague excuse marked by a false kind of prudence. He always felt that in biology, the word "Orthogenesis" must be held on to, along with its meaning: i.e., that life advances in complexity in the direction which ends in man. Here again one sees one of the fundamentals of Teilhard's philosophy: living substance centrates and moves upward toward states whose end and consequence is cephalization. On the other, Teilhard rejected the word "Finality" which has meaning only up to the level of reflection; he preferred the word "Polarity," since there is an interplay of chance between Entropy and Life.

In April Teilhard also attended a three-day meeting at the Academy of Sciences. But if the people were "charming," he found the intellectual atmosphere "suffocating." It was not related disciplines, but the Science of Man and all its ramifications that really interested him. At just this time, another disappointment came. Julian Huxley rejected the paper Teilhard had written for his scientific album on the basis that "it was not written in the same tone as the other papers." Far from taking offense at the refusal (it was not his way), Teilhard replied by insisting that Huxley himself take a stand on the phenomenon of human covergence.

Near Easter, Teilhard visited Childs Frick and met Fairfield Osborn, son of the great paleontologist. On Easter Sunday he went to hear Msgr. Sheen preach in St. Patrick's Cathedral. Though much impressed by the speaker's oratorical gifts, he remarked rather sadly that one of Sheen's strengths was being able to live and see a religion without Mysteries, save those of theology. *"For him,"* he said, *"all is clear, all is sure, all is revealed."*

In this remark one feels again the poignancy of the cry Teilhard made at the end of The Divine Milieu:

"Jerusalem, lift up your head. Look at the immense crowd of those who build and those who seek. All over the world men are toiling—in laboratories, in studies, in deserts, in factories, in the vast social crucible. The ferment that is taking place by their instrumentality in art and science and thought is happening for your sake. Open, then, your arms and your heart, like Christ your Lord, and welcome the waters, the Flood and the sap of humanity."

After the Wenner-Gren conference June 9–20, Teilhard returned to the country to make his yearly retreat. Once more he realized how different was his vision of the world from that of St. Ignatius. In an irreversible way, fixism had given way to movement. Hence the need for searching for a God, both personal and "Ultra-Humanizing" Who, by giving man love as his goal, gives him, in a world where "person" is the most conspicuous expression of creation, the power to surpass himself. This presence of God, the Force behind our evolution in a cosmos where so many contrary forces are at play, is the touchstone of Teilhardian thought. The abandonment of juridicalism, moralism, and all things artificial in order to live in the very function of the call to love by God, Who so elevates our energies, was the heart of his theology.

14 East 71st Street, New York 21, N.Y.
January 13, 1952

Dear Friend,

. . . The Christmas trees and Santa Clauses are gone now, and Valentines are starting to appear. In other words, we're back at work. I'm very happily installed at the Foundation and in my office. I'm composing (for use here and for the Academy in Paris) a note on the Australopithecines. But most important (through what I read in books and through my talks with people) I am trying to clarify my thoughts on the conditions for and the nature of the transformation which will one day move our understanding of the "human phenomenon" out of the domain of "Letters" and into that of "Science."

The other day I received from Professor Northrop (a philosopher and jurist from Yale and one of the pillars of the Foundation) a long and graceful letter indicating that his view of things and mine are diametrically opposed. He considers a fundamental identification between "natural evolution" and "cultural evolution" as purely nominal, while I consider it a fact of experience. I am waiting (and preparing) for an interesting battle at the June symposium—insofar as such a battle can be interesting in view of the humanist-literary character of the participants. I think Fejos is on my side, and I look forward to another symposium on Man when only 10 percent of the participants will be "anthropologists," while the others will be biologists, chemists and astro- or nuclear-physicists. We must talk about this one day....

Otherwise, I'm quite content here in New York which is not at all difficult . . . You know what the weather is like here—the sudden blizzards quickly followed by fine clear, crisp days like those we had at Peking. It's gayer here than it is in Paris. In fact, though I see few people "socially," I dined the other day at Malvina's, and found her just as lively and as sweet as ever. —I should tell you that she will be in Paris in May to supervise the work of her Epinal monument. —Lucile finds her peace in a group directed by a Swami, where Malvina also goes—but only for artistic reasons. The spirituality there seems terribly vague to me. But I wonder if this sort of religiosity may not be the only recourse for those men and women who are unable to pierce the hard envelope that theologians have built around Christianity in the name of "orthodoxy"?—I still have only rare contacts with the Fathers here, especially on the personal level. But that perhaps may come one day. In any case, everybody is pleasant, and I try to be pleasant (if not regular) and above all, not to annoy anybody—as in a regiment one tries to pass unnoticed.

It's not impossible that I will go back to America House some time soon, but that would move me farther from the Foundation. . . .

. . . What has become of Jouve? If by any chance he's still in Paris and does not have a radio, tell him to buy one out of my personal funds. (I've already written Dr. Loriot about this.) I should have thought of this last summer.

Affectionately as ever,
TEILHARD

P.S.

I should tell you that in response to my letter-memoir from Cape Town, Father Janssens very kindly wrote to me, approving my stay here at the Foundation for the time being.

14 East 71st Street, New York 21, N.Y.
January 19, 1952

Dear Friend,

. . . As to my summer projects, which are difficult to change now, I will be going to California in July when New York becomes uninhabited and uninhabitable (Shall I go via Panama?— I'd like to see the Isthmus.), then come back in mid-September. . . .

. . . There's nothing really new here. Yesterday I made contact with another new group (It includes an astronomy professor from Harvard as well as Margaret Mead, the ethnologist) which seems to approach the human problem rather in a direction similar to my own—i.e., as the study of a physical Energy. I'll try to see if they are serious about it. *Apropos* this subject, I'm now reading an interesting book called *Time's Arrow*, by a certain professor Blum (published by the Princeton Press). It's full of interesting facts and ideas about biochemistry and the origins of Life. (It was published in 1951.)

I'm thinking of going to spend some days in Washington in the beginning of February. I particularly want to see people (among them, Ambassador Grew, who helped me, and could help me again) with the bothersome question of visas and their extension.

Best regards to everyone around you at *Etudes* (d'Ouince, Jouve, St. Seine) and at your Lab.

Affectionately always,
TEILHARD

14 East 71st Street, New York 21, N.Y.
February 17, 1952

Dear Friend,

. . . I just got back from Washington (Georgetown University), where I was charmingly received—especially by the rector who once worked on a kind of thesis at the Sorbonne while living on the Rue Raynouard and by Father Walsh (Edmund), the *missus dominicus* of Russia and Japan. At Catholic University, the anthropology department (Father Connolly, a secular priest, and Father Gusinde, a disciple (or rather black sheep) of Father Schmidt, whom I saw this summer at Johannesburg) gave a cocktail party for me, where I met a great many people, notably two brilliant scholastics (one in physics, the other in biology) and among whom I quietly tried to loose my "demon of Research." I also saw people from the Smithsonian (paleontologists and anthropologists); and I dined tête-à-tête with my friends the Grews (the one-time ambassador to Japan, you remember). — The sky was clear and blue over the still-dark trees of the Potomac which will soon burst into bloom. This outing did me considerable good . . . With Connolly, a brain specialist, and Walsh I chatted the longest—and fairly deeply, too, considering that Connolly, like all American Catholics, is still fettered with a style of dogmatic thinking with which we, in France, are no longer occupied; and that Walsh is too involved in Roman politics to take seriously the necessity of a new Catholic Reform (a reform not of discipline or of manners but of our very conception of the Creation, Incarnation and Redemption). —In other words, a new Christology, with Christ drawn to the size and to the organicity of the present universe. As I already told you, as the first step in my new position, I'm trying to make the local anthropologists admit in what precisely the importance and uniqueness of the "human phenomenon" in "Nature" really consists—persuaded as I am that this one match may one day set everything afire—even, and above all, "the bastion" of the Theologians.

To you as ever in deep friendship,
TEILHARD

Thank St. Seine for me for his most interesting letter. Bravo!

14 East 71st Street, New York 21, N.Y.
March 6, 1952

Dear Friend,

. . . Essentially nothing has changed, except that the days are lengthening without notably altering the disorder (to say nothing of the dirtiness) of Central Park. But the greenery, which will hide everything, will soon be with us.

At the Foundation I find more and more to keep me busy, even without the fact that Fejos, at the last moment asked me to write a "preliminary report" on Fossil Man, to be used at the June symposium, in the place of Le Gros Clark, who will be giving conferences in Australia. I intend to write a short presentation, as unpretentious as possible (as I have neither my books nor my papers here), with which I will amuse myself by re-counting the history of the evolution of the notion of Fossil Man from 1850 (when the notion seemed just as unthinkable to biologists as the mutability of the atom seemed to physicists before 1900!) and follow it up to our own time. A complicated, complex notion, interesting to analyze. I'll cover the stages which I myself lived through, when everything in Europe was explained in terms of Neanderthal man, and everything in Asia, in terms of the Pithecanthropus. This unexpected little assignment interests me. But in a sense, I really don't want to do it because so many fascinating books are accumulating on my table, and because, above all, I want to set myself to write two essays which interest me. One will be "The New Anthropology," the other, on what I call "The Reflection (as one speaks of the "conservation" and "degradation") of Energy." I think I already told you about this. But it is getting clearer in my mind. Much of my delay in writing it stems from the fact that between times, I begin to open relations with people who are not interested in Man from a Humanistic or anthropological point of view; for example, John Stuart, director of the Princeton Observatory, and Professor Roger Williams, director of the Institute of Biochemistry in Austin, Texas.—I still don't know what will come of all this, but it lightens the painful atmosphere generated by the "Maccabees" of Ethnology.

Two weeks ago I spoke about the Australopithecines at the Academy of Sciences in New York (a charming setting—the mansion which Barbara Hutton gave to the Academy), and I'm going to speak again next week at the W.G. Foundation, this time on South African prehistory. It's not as easy to do as it would be in French, but I'm trying. Also, Shapiro (the director of the department of anthropology at the Nat. Hist. Museum) has asked me to come and preside once at his seminar. Then there is Ewing from Fordham, who wants to have me for a weekend. Not much time to be bored. . . .

Always affectionately,
TEILHARD

P.S.

   ... All genetic explanation notwithstanding, orthogenesis (as I conceive it) is the established fact that a morphologic "additivity" in a certain direction does exist (for reasons perhaps opposed and variable). Are they a result of inertia or of preference? What, for instance, have hypsodonty* and cephalization in common? I'll take the question up again in another letter....

   ... I had not heard of Licent's death. A real loss, despite everything.

14 East 71st Street, New York 21, N.Y.
March 16, 1952

Dear Friend,

   Here are some more notes to be put with my letter in which I touched on the question of orthogenesis—a subject which interests you at the moment, and about which, as I noticed last Tuesday at Dr. Shapiro's Columbia seminar, many scientists are now asking questions. In my opinion, this is the very place where the problems of evolution arise in their liveliest and most concentrated form. The word "orthogenesis" disturbs and frightens us because we identify it with particular formulae and interpretations, or because the pheonomenon is not easy to interpret in terms of genetics (as we understand it), or because it seems to represent an intrusion into science by philosophy (e.g., the notion of Finality, especially a Finality directed by some creative Idea). But these prejudices simply don't hold up. As I told you, "orthogenesis" (an excellent word to keep in the lexicon, even though it has been much abused, as have "evolution" and "socialism") simply means that, historically, life developed and continues to develop (in ourselves, for instance) *by addition*, or (what comes to the same thing) by continually reaffirming itself

*Hypsodonty: High dentition, as in the molars of herbiferous mammals.

along certain definite lines. In my opinion, this is a fact of pure experience.

To tell the truth, for one reason or another according to the situation, everything which is in *Time* is additive. Entropy is an "additive" progress going toward the more probable.

Life (which "transverses" Entropy) is something very like Entropy;

—*whether we examine it in detail* in each phylum (take hypsodonty* for example). There would be no phyla without "additivity" and it makes no difference that the general phenomenon (as in the case of the equidae) can subdivide into more or less fixed subphyla; the phenomenon manifests itself statistically;

—*or whether we examine it in toto*, as in the whole organic and functional "complexity" along the moving front of Biogenesis.

(N.B., as far as the evolution of the atom is concerned, I don't know whether or not physicists see the formation of the hydrogen-to-uranium scale as a consequence of "additivity." It would be interesting to find out. Probably they're still not sure.)

The point at which the question becomes interesting (from a "*vital*" scientific angle) is when one has to decide whether this "additive drift" of living substance toward more and more complicated states has (or has not) a principal axis leading to cephalization and cerebration. Personally, and all "Philosophy" aside, I see no other way of scientifically identifying the human explosion of the biosphere, or the strange fact that clearly we are still undergoing this drift of cerebration. It is impossible not to go on thinking more and more, and it is impossible not to develop a civilization which will end in the creation of thinking machines to justify it—and perhaps tomorrow, to the undervaluation of our own brains in the process.

All this above could and should be discussed further. But the truth of the existence of this vital phenomenon—if not immediately of a *Finality* (which only appears experimentally with the coming of Reflection, or in Man) but of a *Polarity*—is estab-

---

*Hypsodonty—that phylum characterized by having high or deep crowns and short roots, as the horse.

lished. Vis-à-vis the play of Chance, and thanks to certain basic cosmic curves which we try to recognize and record without being able to explain them any more than we can explain three dimensions of space or the speed of light, we see that the *Weltstoff* is not "isotropic," but that it arranges itself around two principal axes: the axes of greater and lesser probability or the axes of Entropy and Life.

Doubtless, a certain orthogenesis of detail (hypsodonty, for example) can be explained. But general cosmic orthogenesis cannot.

As to what's going on in my own life—all is well. Yesterday I talked at the W.G. Foundation on South Africa, after which I went with my friend Movius* to have a whiskey a few doors away.... Two nights ago I went to a little dinner party with Malvina and Fejos. We missed you!

I'm quite busy now writing my report on Fossil Man for the symposium in June.

Affectionately,
TEILHARD

14 East 71st Street, New York, 21, N.Y.
April 6, 1952

Dear Friend,

Around March 20th, there was a three-day meeting on physical anthropology at the Academy of Sciences in N.Y. Charming people; but an intellectually suffocating atmosphere in the conference room. Endless discussions on deformations of the spinal column, etc. Was it anthropology or orthopedics (?!)— No matter what the cost, we simply must begin work on a real science of the Human Phenomenon! Not an easy thing to do

*Hallam Movius, American Anthropologist and Harvard Professor. Curator of Anthropology at the Peabody Museum from 1957.

though.—In a charming letter Julian Huxley just wrote me that he cannot use the paper I sent him on "the Prolongation of the Process of Evolution in Man" because my pages had not the same tone as the other papers submitted. I answered him at length and most affectionately, that the rejection of my Note is not important; but that, on the other hand, it has become urgent and inevitable for him to take a scientific stand on the physical nature of the irresistible racio-socio-economic-mental Human Convergence which accelerates before our eyes. Yes or no—is this phenomenon of convergence "*eu*-biological" [directed toward a goal] or "*epi*-biological" [undirected]? While any hesitation or equivocation still persists on this point, it is impossible to hope for the conservation of a human "ideology" or the writing of a human "history." (You know from the old days at UNESCO that these subjects are Huxley's two hobbies.) It's interesting to see how much, as much on the right as on the left, the finest minds cannot bring themselves to see in the universe, and especially in Man, this extraordinary—I might say blinding—phenomenon, which Bergson (clearly, although not too scientifically) saw: a Noogenesis* rising through the play of chance. It is a Universe we all experience individually and infinitesimally in ourselves—one which never stops thinking and reflecting more and more (whether because developed arrangement engenders thought or because thought brings about arrangements, I haven't decided, but it's probably a bit of both).— Am I the odd one, or is everyone else blind?—Whatever happens, I'm absolutely determined to press my point at the end.

I've just come back from an overnight stay at the magnificent property of my friend, Frick, on Long Island, where I met Fairfield Osborn (son of the great Osborn and director of the Bronx Zoo) up to his neck now in the question of overpopulation. (He wrote *Our Plundered Planet*.) He's going to France in

---

*Noogenesis: Teilhardian expression for the growth of the "thinking skin" of the earth. Derived from Edouard Suess' definition of its inner core as "Barysphere," its outer envelope as "Lithosphere," and its envelope of living things as the "Biosphere."

May to try to establish ties with biologists there—and incidentally, to study European thought on the "population question". . . .

Frick himself is still digging in three or four locations in the West and in Alaska, accumulating and describing the most astonishing series of Mio-Pliocene mammals I've ever seen. In this collection of skulls and limbs, one can clearly see the formation of "clusters" of neighboring forms (the Camelidae, the Mustelidae, Cyonidae* etc.). Extraordinary material for a paleontological study of the structure of the phylum in "transversal sections"! Speciation in action at a precise time. I don't think that Frick himself will press the study of his collections. But those who work on his collection after will find the material prepared.

At the Congress of Physical Anthropology I had the pleasure of chatting very briefly with Ruth Marzano from Chicago whom you may know from 1950.

. . . I haven't planned anything for Easter except perhaps an appearance at Fordham for a week on "Missionary Ethnology" (!!??). It was difficult to turn down the invitation without seeming a little rude to the Fathers here. Then, too, I have good friends at Fordham.

Very affectionately,
TEILHARD

P.S.

I've definitely made up my mind to go to Berkeley at the end of July until September.

---

*Camelidae: The camel family. Mustelidae: The weasel family. Cyonidae: The dog family.

LETTERS FROM MY FRIEND TEILHARD

14 East 71st Street, New York 21, N.Y.
April 28, 1952

Dear Friend,

. . . What you have written me about Dr. Ockepszye's thesis is utterly bewildering. The only way to understand him is to say that he has taken as a general phenomenon of hominization, a certain residual or *secondary* phenomenon (the divergence and "hardening" of marginal human subphyla which paleoanthropology has, I think, up to now too much confused with the "principal" phenomenon—the complex of elaboration of Homo Sapiens. It's an event which perhaps occupied all of Africa during the Old Paleolithic. I raise this point in my paper for the June symposium. . . .

I passed a quiet Easter here. On Sunday I went to hear Sheen at St. Patrick's. There's no doubt that he's a remarkable orator. (Splendid diction, delivery and feeling.) But he is a man one of whose great strengths lies (as I wrote Jouve) in his being able to see and live a religion without Mysteries (except those of theology). For him, all is clear, all is sure, "all is revealed." All this would be much too beautiful—or perhaps it is not beautiful enough—for the "new God" we await.

As I've had some free time lately, I've written 15 pages on what I call the "Reflection of Energy." Still the same old thing, but pushed a little farther, and better centered in the direction of a general Energetics which composes "spirit and matter" (as we used to say) at the same time. Naturally it's just another paper for me to keep on my desk. If I ever have it mimeographed here, I'll send you a copy.

Now June and the famous symposium are coming. In May I have to go and make a brief trip to Harvard (and perhaps to Yale). Furthermore Simpson is here for a few days and I must see him. All this keeps me occupied.

Recently, and with a great joy, I ran into de Breuvery again. He is here looking for a job in sociology or international relations. We talked a long time, but clearly, he is now much more

"Shanghaian" than Parisian, so I didn't learn much from him about things in France. Right now he is in Washington, but doubtless he'll soon be back and stay at America House. . . . Saw Dr. Loucks again . . . as winning as ever. He left the PUMC last year,* and he's working here on a committee for the Far East. In his opinion the announcement of Vetch's death is premature. All that anyone really knows, he says, is that at the prison, Madame Vetch was told she would not be permitted to return either to bring him things or to visit.

Best regards as ever,
TEILHARD

14 East 71st Street, New York 21, N.Y.
May 24, 1952

Dear Friend,

. . . This morning I leave for Boston (Harvard) for three days. The weekend before I was at Yale where I'd never been before. And to finish my tour of New Haven, I went to spend a day in the Connecticut woods at the home of a curious lady . . . who scientifically and successfully raises turkeys—A lovely "colonial" house, furnished in 18th-century style with furniture, etc., kept in the family (Dutch) for two hundred years. Except for a few rather overpopulated little islands, the countryside around (a granite platform cut by glaciers) is surprisingly untouched. There are trees everywhere, as far as one can see. It was all so pretty under its burgeoning foliage with apple trees and blossoming dogwood!—A kilometer away, there is a very recent foundation of French Benedictine nuns, imported here by an aesthetic lady with the financial aid of Mrs. Luce. (There was a film about the venture recently.)* The convent has a pretty lit-

*Peking Union Medical College, Rockefeller-sponsored Medical Institute in China where the bones of the Sinanthropus were first examined.
*"Come to the Stable." Fox 1949

tle chapel, but already—and as an essential—they've built a great cloister grille.—Alas, alas . . .

And now the famous symposium is upon us. (The 9th to the 20th of June.)—A room as full of communications gadgets as one finds at the United Nations! I don't hope for very much from the conference, which I consider to be ill-recruited. But, loyally, I'll do my best to make it a success. Perhaps one good thing will come out of it—a more scientific and "naturalist" idea of anthropology.—Incidentally, I am still writing some pages on the impossibility (and the danger) of trying to separate biological and human evolution—a thing that American scientists are very stubborn about—at least up to the level of "reflectivity."

Somebody sent me some details on Cognet's book about me. The preface is decidedly sympathetic; but a "Jansenist" like him is the last man in the world I would choose to interpret my "thought," entirely driven as it is by an "optimistic" view of anthropogenesis.—Like a "bottle of champagne," will the opening of that book release a little sigh, or an explosion? I lean toward the theory of the "sigh." In any case, it's a shame I can neither explain nor answer him. It is so evident, as I told somebody recently that the "crux" (or, if you prefer, the Crossroads) of my present situation is my interpretation of "the meaning of the Cross" (in other words the meaning of evil in the world), and my feeling that in the Christianity of tomorrow, the Cross will no longer be only a sign of expiation but a sign of "Evolution" (the emergence of spirit through the play of chance). But how could a Cognet (or a Janssens) deal with that?

I must stop now and pack my bag. De Breuvery is in N.Y. now, settled in America. He's an aide to the French delegation to the United Nations. Through him I've made contact with the French community here. The night before last, I went to a sumptuous dinner at the Lacostes, where I had the great joy of meeting the Hoppenots* again. The party was entirely composed of "Far Easterners"—including Malik (from Russia) who spent a long time in Japan. It was extremely gay and witty. Di-

---

*Henri Hoppenot, French diplomat who served in China before World War II.

rectly imported from Perigord (where Madame Lacoste comes from) they had a foie gras good enough to make one weep.—But I'm just a little old to be a gastronome.

Affectionately,
TEILHARD

14 E. 71st St., NYC 21, N.Y.
June 5, 1952

Dear Friend,

... Received and leafed through Cognet's book. It's kind enough, on the whole. And psychologically he has seen the question (Chapter I) very clearly for an "outsider." But what an *enfant terrible* he is in the frankness with which he pushes the logic of original sin and Christian catastrophism as far as it can go! The categoric affirmation that, historically, humanity reached its high point in some terrestrial paradise and that, since then, Christianity is by nature backward-looking!!!—I really have the impression that the book comes down much harder on the fundamentalists and existentialist Christians than it does on me.

But at least Cognet is frank and logical to the end—at which point one recoils, as before a bad joke.

On a more serious plane. I'm attentively following (*pro modulo meo*) the new ideas about the birth of the cosmos (Hoyle,* etc.) being developed at Cambridge (England) as a corollary to the theory of the expansion of the universe—and in which, incidentally, I will believe only when the idea of the aging of light can be positively excluded. This theory envisages the continuous formation of some kind of protohydrogen which fills the void caused by the expansion of the cosmos. It is curious to con-

---

*Fred Hoyle, 1915/19—) British astronomer. Proponent of the "steady state" theory of the origin of the universe which held that matter is continuously created out of new material.

sider the timing of the announcement of such a theory immediately after the Pope (I wonder who counseled him?) has untowardly engaged his authority to back a proof of God's existence based on "the primitive atom." (!!)—What is most interesting about this work at Cambridge, though, is that it represents one more step taken by science to free itself from old habits of thinking which no one has dared to question for a long time. According to Hoyle, the corpuscular Quantum of Matter forming the Universe is not constant. He holds that there is a current of continuous* intensity in which we are caught up, as by the jet of a fountain. The perspective interests me because, if the Universe were formed in this way, then Spirit, too, would be formed by continuous generation. But how to reconcile this with the existence of a "Divine Foyer" of Cosmic Centration?— Instead of a "Foyer," would we not have a "Line"?—I think I see vaguely that if, in such a universe, consciousness is to be saved biologically all the way, we will have to establish in the system a new curve of another kind (that of the continuous generation of Matter) which would create itself in some kind of "spiral" *around* the Cosmic Foyer of Psychic Reflection, and instead of stretching out in a line, would appear as a continually deepening Center.—But excuse this *charabia*. I'm not exactly writing you a letter right now; I'm only trying to think on someone else's head.

As I told you in my last letter, the symposium opens in three days, and I'll write about it in my next letter. At Harvard ten days ago, I tried out my guns on the relationship between sociology and biology, before a group of some fifteen carefully chosen professors. I think this is the way to go.—In this regard, I was a little perplexed at the gesture of d'Ouince and Rousseau in bringing my paper on the "Reflection of Energy" to the *Revue des Questions Scientifiques*. They didn't understand that all I want-

---

*In modern cosmology, Hoyle's steady state theory has lost popularity to the theory of the "Big Bang," which posits a prima explosion (still in progress) in which subatomic particles fused to form the first hydrogen atoms some 10 billion years ago and sent continually fusing and condensing material into space.

ed was to have some copies of my work for the use of the anthropologists I knew, ordered in Paris. It's not easy to make French polycopies here. The paper was not written for a review or for popular dissemination; but as a "tentative" text for discussion and research. If it lands in Rome, too bad (or so much the better!).

After the symposium I plan to leave N.Y. to spend a week in the country.... If all goes well, I'll go from here to California, and return here about September 1. This summer trip does not especially excite me, but I hope that it will be of some use to me.

> In deep friendship,
> TEILHARD

> 14 East 71st Street, New York 21, N.Y.
> June 27, 1952

Dear Friend,

... Right now—after having gotten out of the symposium alive I'm spending eight days in the country near New York in complete solitude in a wooded countryside, at the very moment when the heat wave arrived in New York. I'm using this calm period for my retreat. The situation is a bit irregular, but I can scarcely arrange things otherwise. I'm sure that St. Ignatius would approve—And speaking of the great Ignatius, I find I can't but realize again (and even more profoundly) the size of the abyss which separates my religious vision of the World and the vision in the Exercises (seen in the mold into which church people in high places still think that we can fit!)—an "abyss" not of contradiction but of expansion. The circle has become a sphere.—Certain conversations which I had at the symposium have confirmed me in my present appreciation of the modern religious situation. Men today, whom circumstances have driven out of the framework of imagination that Theology has built, all are seeking a new God—One who is simultaneously "Personal" and "Ultra-Humanizing" (this last term emphasizes opposition to the fictional "Supernatural" of the Theologians). It is to the understanding of this "Ultra-Christian" God that I am irrevocably determined to devote the last years of my life. I will not, of course, precipitate any rift with the Church; but I'll be only too happy if I have an occasion to "confess" my faith. This does not depend on me, however, but on Him who (I hope) leads me through the jungle.

I plan to leave New York on July 3 . . . and to stop for 24 hours at Simpson's place in New Mexico, and to reach Berkeley on the 10th. I'm hoping to return to New York September 1st via Glacier Park, Montana, where I want to go to see the Pre-Cambrian Collenia* there, and thus complete what China and South Africa have taught me of geology. (What interests me in this, as you know, is the birth of the continents.)

Very affectionately always,
TEILHARD

CALIFORNIA

Teilhard's summer trip was a momentary liberation for him. It brought back memories of other adventures long ago in far-off lands. In the letters he wrote me at that time, there is a vague sense of nostalgia (half-joyous and half-sad) for times and places past. The call of the unknown, the rough life of the camps returned once more. As in the last period in his life, Teilhard tasted again the joy of working in the field. A deep plunge into Nature had always helped to feed his thought and calm his inner life. The visit to Simpson in his adobe house 2,000 miles up in the mountains, the night spent under a tent at the edge of a natural forest where wild turkeys still ventured out to forage, did him good.

---

*Fossilized deposits of calcareous algae, which formed layered mounds with a knobby surface. Individual mounds are 2 to 3 feet in diameter; the grouped mounds form hills covering many acres.

But even more important to his interior growth was his San Francisco visit, where, after contacting a handful of friends from his China years and attending cultural events, he went to see the famous cyclotrons of Berkeley. The experience shook him to the very core. In an essay he wrote about the visit not long afterward, he said that what he ultimately felt before these monstrous engines (these extraordinary products of the "noosphere"), was not terror, but a kind of peace and joy. Joy, because he understood that in order to create the current that was moving mankind both En Haut and En Avant, and to do so with increasing intensity over centuries to come, "the repulsive (or negative) pole of death—if it is to be avoided must, by dynamic necessity be matched by a second, attractive (or positive) pole— the pole of a super life to be attained: a pole capable of arousing and satisfying ever more fully with the passing of time, the two demands characteristic of a reflective activity: the demand for irreversibility and the demand for total unity."

And the more he tried to extend his mind further into the future and into the Divine—into the progress of the immense physico-psychic spiral in which, at that moment, he saw himself historically involved—"the more," he wrote, "it seemed to me that what we still call by the too-simple name of 'research' becomes charged with and warmed with certain forces (such as faith and worship) hitherto regarded as alien to Science." At the same time, he also saw "what we call 'Research' forced by an inner compulsion to concentrate its final hopes and efforts in the direction of a divine center."*

Teilhard's subsequent visit to Glacier Park near the Canadian border added to his experience of geology, by giving him the opportunity of comparing the Pre-Cambrian Collenia there with what he had seen in South Africa and the Far East. From there he turned back east to stay a while at the summer place of friends on an island near Bar Harbor, Maine, where he thought

---

*"En Regardant les Cyclotrons de Berkeley." Published in *Recherches et Debats*, April 1953.

LETTERS FROM MY FRIEND TEILHARD

*over his first year of possibly final exile, and wondered at the
vast differences between the geologic structures of the east and
west coasts of a continent he had crossed in just three days.*

Hotel Durant, 2600 Durant Avenue
Berkeley 4, California
July 12, 1952

Dear Friend,

From my window in the fine sunshine I see the Gulf of San
Francisco—the Golden Gate (and its bridge). It's the first time
that I look at it, knowing that this Door will not open before me
to admit me to the Pacific, where even now I long to go again (if
I can find something to justify it). I got here yesterday from
New York after a trip broken by three successive stops: one in
Chicago in the middle of all the excitement you can imagine on
the very eve of the [Republican presidential] convention (a
whole day at the Hotel Blackstone waiting for the "Super
Chief"); the second, three days at Albuquerque to see the Simpsons; the third, at Los Angeles (a day and a night) where I met
Jean Delacourt, the ornithologist from Clères and Indochina,
who is now a director in the Los Angeles museum.—The stay at
the Simpsons' (George Gaylord, the paleontologist) was very
pleasant and picturesque. He and his wife lived at an altitude of
8,000 ft. at the edge of a natural forest, three hours by automobile from Albuquerque, in full view of the badlands of the
San Juan Basin. This winter wild turkeys foraged all around
their house.—I stayed in a tent. . . . In a short time I learned a
great deal of geology and cemented my friendship with the
Simpsons. (All this could have important consequences for the
birth of "the New Anthropology.") Then here at Berkeley I ran
into a whole series of dear friends: R.W. Chaney, still astonished
at the discovery of the metasequoia that he found in Szechuan
(he seems to go to Japan every six months), Charles Camp with
whom I examined the material brought back from South Africa

in 1947, Ruben Stirton, very absorbed in the exploitation of a quite fine Myocene basin in Colombia, South America (the fauna is just as fine as Patagonia).—I plan to stay here until mid-August, and then go to Glacier Park, Montana, to see the American Pre-Cambrian Collenia formations*—I plan to come back to New York toward the first of September.

The famous June symposium generated much more heat than light. Still, I think the effort (a very large effort) will have some results—at least in terms of acting as an incentive. But my experience is that anthropology, if it is to continue as a science—and more than that, if it wants to begin to live—must leave the schools of Letters and Medicine behind. Man can only be understood through tracing his rise through Physics, Chemistry, Biology and Geology. In other words, man is a *cosmic* phenomenon, not *primarily* an aesthetic, moral or religious one. It is mind-boggling to think how little this elementary thesis still is understood (it is, however, just beginning to be glimpsed) by the finest minds. . . .

From the 20th of June to the 3rd of July, I went to relax in the Strauses' admirable suburban country house . . . where in absolute calm I even made what I consider a sufficient "retreat." I still don't entirely understand where life is leading me; but at least it seems that there is in me a growing thrust upward toward some kind of total picture. It's still the same old thing, but growing clearer and more serene, because more sure (perhaps) in me, all the time.—I'll explain this to you some day when we meet again.

Here in San Francisco, I just talked by telephone with Jacques Bardac [from China] whom I'm going to see next week. He seems perfectly happy and so does Marie-Claire. Laurens-Castellet has just left. I miss him a little.

> Very affectionately,
> As ever,
> TEILHARD

*Collenia formations—fossilized deposits of calcareous algae, which form layered mounds with a knobby surface.

LETTERS FROM MY FRIEND TEILHARD

P.S.

Would you send, or have [Brother] Cochet (to whom I send my greetings) send to Camp 2 or 3 copies of my "Titres and Travaux" adding to them whatever you find of the tear sheets printed in the *Revue des Questions Scientifiques* and in the *Société de Géologie* in my *dépôt* at *Etudes*? Thank you.

Berkeley, July 30, 1952

Dear Friend,

Thank you for your letter of the 14th. I was deeply pained to hear of the sudden passing of Cosme.* (I immediately . . . gave the news to Jacques who was very sad to hear it. Cosme helped him quite a bit, and he has not forgotten.)—Also, a note from Madame Vaufrey told me that Jouve is in the Rue Oudinot (always that Rue Oudinot!!) with a heart attack.—I wonder what tomorrow holds for him. Whatever happens, I am sure he will deal with it as well as possible.—But where can he be placed where he will still feel alive? At times like this he must (as must we all) take the difficult step into the "Unique Consistent," the "One Thing Necessary."

Here I continue to lead an interesting life in an admirable setting—at least since the fog has lifted. I've seen Jacques and Marie-Claire many times, most memorably for an extraordinary dinner in their very pretty house. Jacques has not grown old, and Marie-Claire is as young as ever. . . . In fact, if anything, I have too many invitations as I try to establish new contacts. I often go (yes, me!) to the Chinese restaurants of San Francisco, which seem to put me right back in the atmosphere of Peking and Shanghai. And three days ago, Goldschmidt, the geneticist, brought us to a Hungarian concert (a quartet) at Mills College in Oakland, where rich Californian girls go, and where I made the acquaintance of Darius Milhaud in person. (He alternates his

*Vichy Ambassador to China during World War II and Teilhard's close friend.

138

time between Paris and San Francisco—one year here and one year there.) He told me that he is working steadily on the opus of his life: a lyrical composition ordered by Israel for its third millennium: the anniversary of David and the foundation of Jerusalem. He is a very likeable man who made me think of Grosbois. It seems that he (or at least his wife) knows my papers!

Every morning I go to the department of paleontology at Berkeley to refresh my mind on a few points. Chaney has left. But Camp is still here and so is Stirton who really runs things. Under his direction, Berkeley is rapidly becoming the best center of paleontological stratigraphy (or of stratigraphic paleontology) in the world. In the domain of fossil mammals, the laboratory is above all busy with the exploitation of a great Miocene basin which was found in Spanish Colombia during the war, and which completes, in a very useful way, the data that up until now came only from Patagonia.

Beyond my own specialty, I've been able (thanks to the patronage of Chaney who bizarrely enough, was part of that atomic energy committee during the war) to visit the great cyclotron of the university, in function and in construction the largest in the world. And, incidentally, as I wrote to Russo, while I was there, I received exactly the shock that I expected. Faced with this incredible apparatus, one has the feeling of losing one's footing in the human. At this level, everything comes together: the laboratory industry, war and even somehow, the highest kind of philosophy. (I mean the search for a first or last Element in things.) And what can one say of the scale and complexity, the technique and the calculi of which these great monsters are made—and also of the population of engineers and physicists consistently employed in the effort to tend them?—A new Humanity is being born by the natural force of events, which cries out (I feel it more and more strongly) toward and for a "new" God.—As I look toward these extraordinary products of the "noosphere," I cannot but believe that tomorrow it will be devices of this kind which will be employed to control Life or the new biology. And doubtless, it is in prolongation of the same movement of recasting and generally rethinking the world, through the bases which constitute it, that at last a Science of Man, less ridiculous than the one which burdens us at this moment, will emerge. . . .

. . . I plan to leave Berkeley on August 8th, to go for five days to Glacier Park (Montana) to see the Pre-Cambrian Collenia there, then to continue on to Maine (to the summer place of R.'s sister and brother-in-law) and to come back to my office at the Wenner-Gren Foundation around September 1st. In the course of the next year, I would like to start some kind of symposium project (one that would be restricted, and very select) on the definition of a new and truly scientific anthropology. During that time I hope Rome will leave me in peace.—No news at all on that side. I won't be the one who makes the first move.

Most affectionately yours,
TEILHARD

THE RETURN TO NEW YORK

In the beginning of September, Teilhard was back at his desk at the Wenner-Gren Foundation in New York. His exile weighed ever more heavily upon him. Even though the new superior at St. Ignatius, Robert Gannon, was kind to him and gave him all the liberty that he needed, he was unhappy in a house in which there was no other Jesuit with whom he could truly share his thoughts.

About this time, he heard that the University of Laval at Quebec was preparing a congress on Evolution to which the most celebrated paleontologists had been invited. Simpson had already announced, with an ironic smile, his imminent descent upon the conference. Through other channels Teilhard heard that Rome was sending a Jesuit professor from the Pontifical University in Rome (a man whose views were as distant as possible from evolutionist opinion) to represent the Catholic point of view. And yet, no one even considered inviting him. Although he treated the matter fairly lightly, one may imagine his interior distress.

140

About the same time, a congress of humanists met in Amsterdam to discuss the meaning of Man. In Teilhard's mind, such literary-philosophic conventions only clouded the subject further. Doubtless the delegates discussed the possibility of man's action upon evolution, but upon evolution that had no soul or any stimulus other than its own physical and intellectual betterment. For whom should it be better? And why? To all of this they had no answer.

But long ago Teilhard had said what he thought: "Because I have looked so long at Nature, and loved her face so much that I can read her heart, it is my dear, profound conviction—a conviction as sweet as it is tenacious, the humblest but the deepest of my certitudes. . . . Life does not go off on any road at all. Neither does it misjudge its End. . . . It shows us by what route will come all those who are neither liars nor false gods; it shows us toward what point on the horizon we must steer if we are to see the Light arise and fill the sky."*

On September 20, 1952, Teilhard learned of the death of his old friend, Raymond Jouve, after a long and painful sickness during which he had almost completely lost his eyesight. Jouve had been a man of decision and great intellectual openness whom Teilhard held in high esteem. The loss cut deeply.

But one of his consolations during his visit to America was that he had with him at St. Ignatius Père Emmanuel de Breuvery. He greeted his arrival with delight, and through the years which they would pass together under the same roof, Teilhard admired his courage and savoir faire.

In 1952 Teilhard's idea of "reforming" anthropology took shape. The Wenner-Gren Foundation agreed to a campaign to support and integrate research projects concerning human origins. It therefore seemed possible that Teilhard might come to Europe that summer on his way to South Africa. Unfortunately, the hope proved to be illusory.

---

*"La Vie Cosmique" collected in *Ecrits du Temps de la Guerre*, Editions du Seuil, Paris, p. 22.

LETTERS FROM MY FRIEND TEILHARD

At about this time, the American political scene was domi-
nated by the victory of Eisenhower over Stevenson in the race
for the presidency. The fact worried Teilhard. What he feared
was that the Republican victory would mean a new rise of the
worst kind of capitalism, whose demands and reactionary views
could not be reconciled with the aspirations of a growing world.
Human society has, over the last century, been more and more
caught up in a yearning for true justice. It is therefore indis-
pensable that "liberalism" be understood not as opening the
way to more and more substantial gains at the expense of the
less fortunate, but as liberation from the bonds in which too
many people are still held. This distress on Teilhard's part
about social ideas, which is evident in some of his political com-
ments, quite logically corresponds to the idea of an "evolution"
in the reorganization of the distribution of goods.

And speaking of liberty, events in America after the presi-
dential inauguration justified Teilhard's uneasiness. The ongo-
ing anticommunist campaign of Senator Joseph McCarthy and
his cohorts seemed to find encouragement in the coming of the
Eisenhower regime. After the election, McCarthy stepped up
his efforts, and sadly enough, as Teilhard noted, "the great mass
of American Irish Catholics seemed to support him."

This section of Teilhard's letters to me ends with one writ-
ten on New Year's Eve, in the middle of the New York Christ-
mas celebration which he found simultaneously quaint and
childlike. Despite the traditional preparations for the holiday,
the exuberance of the crowds, the kindness of his friends, the
various gifts people gave one another, he was regretful at not be-
ing able to feel what was expected of him. He did, however, go
to Midnight Mass in St. Patrick's Cathedral—and one can imag-
ine in what state of mind. Profoundly persuaded as he was of
the truth of his "gospel," "this great fresco of the world" which
both his science and his prophetic intuition had designed made
the trees and the holly and the general mutual goodwill seem
small indeed. Teilhard's vision illuminated the mystery of the
Incarnation in quite another way.

14 East 71st Street, New York 21, N.Y.
September 9, 1952

Dear Friend,

. . . Since the fifth of the month I've been reestablished here
at the Foundation and also at my room in the Jesuit residence on
Park Avenue. There is a new superior* there, a kind of friend,
who, while he was Rector of Fordham in 1948, invited me to
dine as guest of honor (a thing which rarely happens to me) with
a group of his professors at the Century Club.—Fejos is away at
the Congress of Anthropology in Vienna (a vague, rather
"Schmidtian" affair to which the Foundation first tried to send
me but from which I was able to extricate myself). As soon as he
gets back, I plan on bringing up certain problems with him, regarding the "reform" of anthropology. I'll tell you about it later.

I'm not sure when I wrote you last. (From Berkeley on August 30?) But I should tell you the last lap of my trip was most
successful. At Glacier Park, Montana (on the Canadian border),
thanks to the Chief Naturalist there and the presence of a young
naturalist from the French National Survey, I was able to see
everything I wanted to of the Collenia. I'm going to send a paper with some observations about it (comparisons with China
and the Transvaal) to the French Geological Society and to the
Institute.—Luckily the weather was magnificent. In this
countryside of great mountains and great forests, we stayed
eight days in the cabins of Lake MacDonald. There was of
course a flood of tourists.—At the end of the trip, I went to
spend ten days in a cabin in the middle of the woods on the edge
of a kind of fjord.—Four or five years ago the island (and Cadil-
lac Park as well) was ravaged by a terrible fire which partially
destroyed the Genetics Laboratory at Bar Harbor (that's the
place where they raise purebred mice for the world market—
you must have heard mention of it somewhere). In any case, it
was an entirely level plateau surrounded by mountains.—I was

*Robert Gannon, S.J.

much impressed at being able, within a few days' time, to compare the West and East Coasts of the U.S. Geologically, it's the difference between night and day.

Apparently, I'm going to spend the year in New York preparing for a new voyage (to Africa? by way of Europe?) for next year. Père Ravier, my provincial wrote me a fine letter—the best I ever received from any superior in the Company. But there's nothing in it that signals a green light to go back to Paris.—Just last week, I learned that the University of Laval at Quebec is about to hold a congress on Evolution. Naturally, no one has thought (or dared) to ask for a contribution from me. But I know that Simpson is going ("to see the dope," he says). Piveteau was also invited (I wonder if he'll go. I hope so.), as was Boyer (?!)* to represent Rome and save philosophy.—These Catholic-scientific events are touching as displays of good will; but a little ridiculous—a desperate attempt to seem as though they are in the lead, without taking one step forward.—Yesterday when I read the Pope's discourse to some visiting astronomers (they're having a congress in Rome) I had the same impression. It was as if the Pope and the astronomers had an invisible wall between them which made them as much strangers to one another as if they lived in different worlds—people juxtaposed and looking at the same thing, but each seeing something different.—On the Pope's side, still this terrible "extrinsicism" which visualizes God as an Architect, and Man (in a strange return to the 16th century, but exaggerated in reverse) no longer as the center of the Universe, but as a grain of sand "corrected" by intelligence which entered it, one knows not whence, but of course through the intervention of the Architect.

All this makes silence difficult. Above all when, in the face of these Catholic games, one sees the clouds that have gathered over the Congress of Amsterdam. I wrote a long letter to Huxley (a very moderate and sympathetic one, of course) observing that his efforts to establish a new religion would not jell until he

---

*Charles Boyer, Franco-Roman theologian of the Academy of St. Thomas, member of the Holy Office.

defined more clearly the essence of Hominization—and even more, unless he recognized an Issue or Foyer of "Ultra-Personalization" at the end of Anthropogenesis. When Evolution becomes reflective, I told him, it can then only function in a Universe whose nature is generally definable as loveable and loving. This is not a question of sentiment but of pure Energetics. Christianity discovered that 2,000 years ago; and it is this that has established its irreplaceable ascendancy, so long as no one finds anything better in the same direction.

In fact, all this gives me an urge to write and cry the very simple thing I see: a synthesis (of the same Christic stuff) between the old *En Haut* and the new *En Avant*—this very *En Avant* that Rome will not have. For if the pope seems to be moved by the immensity of Space, on the other hand, he has no sense of its fearful and admirable organicity. I'll continue to write, of course.

As ever in Christ,
TEILHARD

P.S.

The last "word" from the Theologians (*Time* Magazine 15–8–52)! *Apropos* of flying saucers—Father O'Connell, a Redemptorist and dean of the Catholic School of Sacred Theology: "These rational beings (the flying saucer passengers) have never committed original sin. That's to say, if they possess the immortality of the body once enjoyed by Adam and Eve, it would be foolish of our pilots to try to kill them. They would be unkillable." Fr. O'Connell may be a pretty cool joker; but in just a few words, he has succeeded in reducing the very essence of the "Theology" of the Fall to complete absurdity.

LETTERS FROM MY FRIEND TEILHARD

New York, September 29, 1952

Dear Friend,

Thank you for your letter telling me about the death, or rather the deliverance, of dear Jouve. It makes a terrible void in my life.—With you and after you, he was one of the few Jesuits to whom I could say everything, sure of being understood—yes, and yes again, there is Only One Thing Necessary ... You speak to me of the flame of the priesthood, and you are right. But in what, precisely, does the composition, the temperature, and the intensity of this flame consist? I was thinking the other day (*apropos* of the feast of Isaac Jogues and Brébeuf) that right now while the idea of "propagating" anything leaves me completely indifferent, I am uniquely and entirely fascinated by the idea of "discovering" God, in what I call "the Christ Universal." I cannot lift up my head or my heart while the Christian message has (due to a deficiency of expression) lost so large a part of its "pull" upon souls. This is a thing which must be restored and reformed, and even more, recast in a fuller dimension, so that it can spread again and take fire spontaneously.—Incidentally, did I tell you that answering an explicit invitation of Father Ravier of Lyon, I wrote and sent him some pages on this subject which I called "Le Sens de la Croix"?

And did I also tell you that my work here seems about to straighten out? The Foundation (a little at my own urging) seems decided to concentrate its efforts upon a "campaign to support and integrate researches concerning human origins in central and southern Africa." In this affair, if it does take shape, I will serve as Fejos's first lieutenant—first here, and then in Africa. In order to do this (and in order to work on the "reform of Anthropology"), if only I were ten years younger.—Still no response from Huxley whom I tried to contact to help me in my efforts to reunite man's biology. Intellectually, he is pretty hard to pin down (Huxley, I mean) but he has warmth and prestige, and I think we like each other very much.

De Breuvery just arrived at the Park Avenue residence,

146

which is extremely pleasant for me. He wants to join an international economics section at the United Nations, which would be splendid.

But would you believe that one of the only hitches which remain to the project is the question of wearing a Roman collar (!!!)—a point on which Spellman is absolutely intractable. O monumental and too-significant stupidity!—Nevertheless, tomorrow (I think) the luminaries at the University of Laval in Quebec are getting together to see whether or not "the earth turns," in other words, if there's such a thing as evolution. Out of coquetry (or maybe bluff) they have invited some well-known non-Catholics—among them. Simpson (who accepted with a smile in his pointed beard, in order "to see the dope"). Piveteau was invited. Will he go?

I've a feeling that I've perhaps only given you a part of the news. Oh, well!—Write me about your plans, and about our friends. Still no news about Lejay.

Most affectionately,
TEILHARD

New York, October 14, 1952

Dear Friend,

... Don't you think that the present oscillations in the world between spiritualism and "pantheism" (or better still, personalism and "pantheism"—which must not be confused with "spiritualism" and "materialism") are less the proof of the instability of the modern mind than they are the sign that Cuénot (like so many others—and even me, in my way) was not able to find around him (and for good reason) the form of expression of the God Whom he interiorly adores: a God in Whom the Christ of Evolution, the Personal and the Universal, the *En Haut* and the *En Avant* are all joined? From this point of view, I insist Cuénot was not a waverer, but religiously, "a man without a country," through the very excess of his religious need, a remarkable biological example of the new type of Believer which is being born in humanity in this moment. But perhaps all this is just "my own invention."

Here life continues. De Breuvery has decidedly joined the United Nations—collar and all. As a matter of fact, he's absolutely alone in an alien milieu: the only Christian among thirty unbelievers making up his "department." It's an unheard-of adventure which he will pull himself through more perfectly than he knows, even with his charm and economic contacts. I'm delighted to have him at Park Avenue in the same house with me.

At the Wenner-Gren Foundation, the great project of African research into human origins seems to be taking shape. And if things continue to go well, it's possible that I'll go to Europe this summer to a conference (in London). We have to have a small meeting of the general staff toward the end of the month.

All this, I repeat, does not distract me from my other objective: the reform of Anthropology and the reform of Christology (no less!). It is disquieting to see both here and in Rome the multiplication of emotional "Marial" rallies at which they cry "Death to Materialism!" never dreaming that for us (those of us who believe in cosmogenesis) there's no such thing as "pure matter" or "pure spirit," that the only way of conquering communism is to present Christ as He is, not as an opiate (or derivative) but as the essential Mover of a Hominization, which can only be achieved energetically in a world both "amorized" and open at the summit. Oh, what a need I have to cry these elementary things!—But how?

TEILHARD

New York, November 5, 1952

Dear Friend,

. . . Let me try to make you understand me better.—Are you really quite sure that from now on, there is not something *more*

148

(and in a sense, *beyond*) the God of the Christians and Philosophers, and the God of the Physicists and the Naturalists (who no longer are in any sense the "savants" of Pascal's time)? Quite literally, I, too, admit that "savants" are priests, and that research is prayer (perhaps the highest kind of prayer). The drama of Cuénot and so many others is not that they turn their backs on Metaphysics, but that they are turned *toward* Evolution's "Convergence on itself" and on its fundamental drive toward the Personal and toward "ultra-personalization." This is a pantheism of diffusion, or at least of divergence. Could they but see things in a *convergent* form (as everything in the phenomenon forces us to), then all false problems of Transcendence and Finality would be dissipated, and they would be able to adore.— Yes, do a little thinking yourself about the real existence and the attributes required by such a "God of the Naturalists". . . .

Here in America, the whole country is relaxing after the success of Ike—a disconcerting thing for intelligent people, but an event which was psychologically inevitable since he (Ike) promised the voters the moon (he said he would go personally to Korea to "bring home the boys!")—In any case, the prestige of a hero may yet have a great advantage in Europe and in Russia.— But this success means a return of hope to the great financiers, who still think they can control the unions. Will the triumph of Ike draw in its wake a dangerous renaissance of capitalism (in the worst and most reactionary sense of the word)? That is the real question. And naturally all the clergy are behind him—on the usual tight rein, of course.

For me the next two weeks will be busy and interesting.— This evening I met Kobayashi at Columbia. Tomorrow and Saturday we're having meetings of the general staff (the five of us) to discuss African projects at the W.G. Foundation. From the 13th to the 15th I'm going to Boston to the annual meeting of the Geological Society of America. I'll tell you all about it in my next letter.

> With deep friendship,
> TEILHARD

LETTERS FROM MY FRIEND TEILHARD

New York, November 26, 1952

Dear Friend,

Every day I'm more and more convinced that it is really by accord between the two terms (or biological functions) of hominization and speciation, or (what comes to the same thing) by the accord between the two terms of socialization and speciation, that one may (and then only) "break the glass" between anthropology and biology—as well as (but that's another story) break the glass between anthropology and Christology. Naturally, it's not a question of reducing hominization to simple animal speciation, but of *generalizing* the notion of speciation. In other words, as I see it, there is only one "evolution of Speciation"— just as there is only one "evolution of Finality"—or of "invention," etc. What I see as the vice of all the neofinalists (Ruyer, etc.) is their desire to find "finality" comparable to human "intention" existing from the time that life began—from the very beginning, I repeat. This smacks of anthropomorphism in the worst sense of the word.

Otherwise things continue normally. I went to Boston for the annual meeting of the Geological Society of America—a bit of a mob scene, some 3,000 participants! But I did manage to make a few interesting contacts. Simpson was awarded the Penrose gold mdeal.—Some days before (I can't remember whether or not I wrote you this) we had a meeting of the General Staff of six at the Foundation to lay out the first plans for "Operation Africa." All went very well. A second meeting is planned for London in July. If all goes well (and if the Mau Mau become a little more tranquil) I'll go from London to Kenya to "observe" and act as liaison. It should be about a three-month trip. Don't talk about this much to those around you. P. Ravier has granted me all necessary permissions.

I sent a slightly fanciful (but basically serious) article to Barrat ("Intellectuels Catholiques Français") on this whirlwind of research called "While Contemplating the Cyclotrons of Berkeley." I don't know if he'll use it. I'm also thinking of sending *Etudes* a few pages (not yet written) on the End of the human species—rather disguised as an apocalyptic piece and quite explicit on the Marxist-humanitarian myth of the Golden Age before us. The burden of it is that what, objectively speaking, seems most naturally to be the goal of speciation is a Second Breakthrough of Species. But will *Etudes* accept it? Well, we'll see.

Meanwhile, J. Huxley sent me the text of his lecture in Amsterdam on "Evolutionary Humanism." In it, I saw with satisfaction that (without naming me) he accepts my views on the special character represented by the human species, in that it does not "split into wholly separate groups or species," but groups itself into "a single inter-thinking group."—But he refuses to go any further.—And instead of considering, as I do, the probability of a Pool of Convergence before us, he only speaks of a "common pool of shared thought and ideals." In other words, he implicitly refuses to take the famous step of placing hominization (or culturation) and speciation in the same general mechanism. And the result is a cloudy and inefficient "*Weltanschauung*" (as somebody clearly told him).

Tomorrow (Thanksgiving Day) I will doubtless go to have turkey and pumpkin pie in the Strauses' lovely country house at Purchase near here. The weather looks miserably gray. Otherwise, I see few people (socially).—But I don't miss it.—And already the department stores are decorated for Christmas!

Now I'll pass on to you what's new here in politics. A complete crisis of reaction has begun to show itself anti-New Deal and anticommunism—with, unhappily (except for *AMERICA* of which the Order seems a bit ashamed), the great mass of Irish Catholics enthusiastic for McCarthy and Co. It's so easy to be "anti." It quite dispenses one from thinking.—But why the deuce must the Church (which alone, I think and proclaim, is capable of keeping the Universe "open" and "warm") present itself right now (through its official authority and through the attitude of its average adherents) as the most redoubtable force of inertia slowing down "hominization"?—I was thinking of this again recently in reading the articles of PP. Tesson and

Beirnaert in the November *Etudes*. All that energy wasted in painfully doing an exegesis of the recent pontifical oracles!— And pity the poor readers who wander bewildered through these distinctions where there is nothing constructive or nourishing to be found.

Most affectionately always,
TEILHARD

New York, December 24, 1952

Dear Friend,

... I am extremely disappointed by what is being written in Catholic magazines this month for the centennial of St. Francis Xavier. This date should be the occasion for casting a more thoughtful look on the modern problem of the Conversion of the World than that of the 16th century missiology. Of all people, you and I know just how much (despite a few admirable points) what is now happening in the Far East can be called "a triumph for the Cross!"—To which remark of mine, I know you would answer that a *serious* article on the question would be unprintable.—But isn't this precisely the ill from which we suffer? An official church which accuses the world of growing tepid while it is really they, the leaders, who are letting the "God of the Gospel" (who by nature and in order to remain Himself, must become the "God of Evolution") grow cold in their hands.—I say this without bitterness. You know that such a bitterness would be impossible to me, so certain am I that the "ever-greater God" is going to arise irresistibly, or even more, perhaps has already shown himself.

And here we are on Christmas Eve. You can imagine the state of excitement and the touching "mutual good will" in this great city of New York which is simultaneously so sophisticated and so childlike. . . . I do my best to put myself in the Christmas spirit. But it does not come easily to an Auvergnat Teilhard.

152

The thing that keeps me from feeling anything is basically (as one of the most Teilhardian and the most intelligent of my uncles used to say in the presence of certain emotional manifestations) that all the fuss here "makes me gag."—But not completely. The proof: I go tomorrow to High Mass at St. Patrick's. I like the church, the location; and the music is quite nice.

On December 29th I have to go to Philadelphia on the occasion of the meeting of the Congress of American Physical Anthropologists. Dr. Fejos is going to hold a private meeting of his own there to press forward the plans for "Operation Africa." All this looks hopeful: some practical work (at vital points) is already in course in Kenya and Angola and the Transvaal. The whole thing is taking shape.—Yes, if only I were ten years younger!—But is not making the act of communion with time the supreme form of adoration?—Naturally I will keep you up to date on my projects of the summer when they are more definite.

Happy New Year.

> And most affectionately always,
> TEILHARD

1953

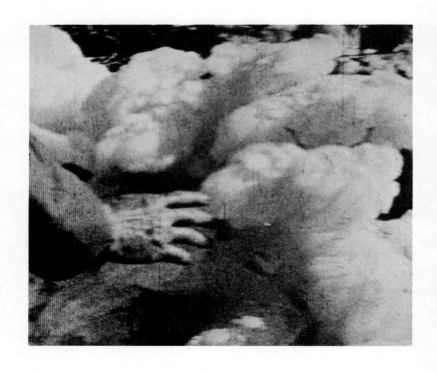

Teilhard's hand dislodging ice crystals after ice storm on a field trip in China

*I*n the first half of 1953 my friend was not at all well. His letters all seem weighted with a kind of mental fatigue, due as much perhaps to poor health as to that purifying inner suffering that he, like all great souls, endured from time to time. In such moments he was tormented by inexplicable crises of anxiety, during which he lived more in perplexity than assurance and during which even the smallest events took on inordinate importance. When such seizures took him (as well I remember from China and later from France), he would wrap himself in silence, to the bafflement of those around him. Though he was prevented by his characteristic reserve from giving voice to his pain, his face always stiffened with a curious austerity, and so concentrated on his inner world did he seem, that one would think the world outside no longer existed. At such times he was forced to live to a profound degree that doctrine of renouncement which enabled him to embrace the terrifying Darkness and trust himself to the Mercy that he neither saw nor felt.*

But even at the worst of times, Teilhard never thought or wrote that he was tired of living. He made his own the imperative of Gogol: "Be ye risen souls, and not dead souls; there is no other way out than that indicated by Christ Jesus." He tried to concentrate more deeply on his old conviction that if he was really to love the world, it was his duty, rather than turning his back on the Earth, to utilize everything—good or bad—that came to him.

Furthermore, even in these moments of depression, he made it a point to keep on writing. This time, and out of his bitter interior emptiness, he forced himself to write an essay on "The Future of Man," and to send to Jean-Marie Le Blond, the director of Etudes, *his reaction to an article that appeared in that journal on "Atheism and the Collège de France." He also reflected on and finally wrote an article on "Culturation and Speciation." Immersed as he was then in anthropology and geology, Teilhard could not possibly keep abreast of all the new aspects of biology, but that did not keep him from thinking on it. In the letter that he wrote me on May 6, for example, he addressed himself to the still-open question of how socialization contributes to the evolution within species. He puts the question of how, within a species, the common fund of ideas, techniques and individual aspirations which is used for the betterment of the group, is written into the genetic code and passed on to descendants. After habits are acquired, are they or are they not, coded into chromosomes?*

In his opinion, "that accumulation of certain things acquired" is the very essence of evolution. Before such an affirmation, the "dogmatic"biologist frowns in bewilderment. Neo-Darwinsim recognizes very few factors in the evolvative process. For the most part, it calls upon mutations (the fruit of the play of chance) that happen when genes are mixed together in a pool. For neo-Darwinists, it is selection which makes the favorable choice. In my opinion, it is, however, important to explore the meaning of "things acquired" in Teilhard's sense. What does the term represent? Is it, as seems logical, linked to molecular structure? The problem still is unsolved.

Furthermore, if, as Teilhard would wish, the modern biologist were to admit the existence of a certain "energy of evolution," he must also wonder how it acts and how it is inscribed in the chromosomes of those new organisms whose behavior depends on their genetic inheritance. The problem of defining the notion of an energy of evolution scientifically still remains. Naturally, Teilhard did not in his correspondence try to answer questions as complex as this. He did not define; he suggested. In the same way as, when he wrote The Phenomenon of Man *in 1939–40, he proposed a strict distinction between tangential energy (e.g., thermodynamics) and "radial energy" (e.g., psychic energy), and placed in relief the two main characteristics of the living being, so by the time he wrote me the letter of May 6, 1953, he seemed to be trying to detach himself a little from this hypothetical distinction. At that point in his life he was concerned about devoting himself to a more general kind of Energetics, a discipline which he saw as the basic condition for the "valorization" and "amorization" of the world.*

But what does it mean: to "amorize" the world? To Teilhard it meant exciting minds and hearts, and inspiring mankind to that simultaneously intellectual and moral action without which Evolution at this level would come to an abrupt end. On this level he attributed to Christ the preponderant influence, thus removing the whole question from the strict domain of science. Though science is only interested in "material" phenomena, Teilhard always saw "material" phenomena as impregnated with "spirit." For him, it was the major theme, the foundation of the cosmic and human edifice.

Another question that lingered in Teilhard's mind at that time came from his contacts with biologists, both Christian and non-Christian. It was the problem of the attitude that men engaged in the laboratory should have. Shut up in their specialty, prying with success and conscientiousness into the details of the biological process, most of them seemed to miss that one dimension that would give meaning to their work—that deeply moralizing and spiritualizing force which bears the study of life forward. They did not search beyond phenomena for life's real meaning, whence came disappointment and a question: has research any other value than its own efficacity? It is a question to which Teilhard himself replied: "Research is the evolvative act par excellence. Destined one day to become the essentially human act, it is the most direct form of Christification and adoration."

At that time, there was also a certain tendency in the Church to criticize the presence of the priest in the laboratory. Many people thought that priests engaged in science somehow diminished their primary function: that of giving God to man. Teilhard held a contrary opinion. "We priests, we Jesuits," he said to a world meeting of Jesuits at Versailles in 1947, "must believe in research because research (pursued with 'faith') is the very terrain fit for the growth of the humano-Christian mystique that can create human unanimity."*

In the course of a conversation I had once with him, the question once arose, "If you were elected pope, what would be your first encyclical?" He answered without hesitation, "It would be on the meaning of Progress."

January 26, 1953

Dear Friend,

What has become of you? It is so long since my last letter to you on December 24. . . .

Since the New Year, nothing noteworthy has happened. As usual, I divide my time between the Foundation . . . and Park Avenue. I continue to mull over the relationship between "culturation" and "speciation," and also to quietly pursue the development of the Africa project.—In this area, things progress (concrete projects for digs, reports received, etc.) If only everything on the continent is not destroyed in the present political-racial tumult!—And speaking of traveling to Africa, I finally had to give up the idea of going to Kenya because I realized that

*"La Valeur Réligieuse de la Recherche," written at St. Germain–Laye in August 1947.

even if I went by boat, I would have to be inoculated against yellow fever again—a thing I prefer not to do since my adventure of 1947*. (Probably the connection between the injection and the *infarctus* was coincidence, but I can't be sure.) And then there is the Mau Mau problem.—So I'll probably content myself with work in the Union of South Africa—which means that I must change all my plans. For example, instead of passing quickly through France (a thing I rather worried about because it could be more tiring and painful now than pleasant) I will go directly from New York to Cape Town at the end of June, if all goes well.—In that case, I will hope to come and stay a few months in Paris in 1954.—But all this is still quite vague. So keep it for yourself.

Otherwise, I continue to write a little (most recently a few pages on "Human Compression)." Did I tell you that *Etudes* did not dare to accept my little article on "The End of the Species"? They can't find anything precise to say about it, but doubtless they are afraid of awakening one of the so-sensitive eschatologists.—[Incidentally, an article on the Church that appeared in *Etudes* recently made me wish we could profess a more objective "hymn," exalting what is modern and irreplaceable in the Christic vision and in the "Christian phylum". . . .]

Even outside the Church, Man is not considered a simple isolated unity, for pity's sake!—And I'm the first to admit that Cosmic Union can only be achieved in the Christic Foyer. But the process leading to this Union begins lower down. Even on the zoological level, the human species converges.

And, *apropos* of the Human, have you seen Charles Darwin's last book *The Next Million Years?* It's a kind of Darwinism, pushed to the extreme, without, unhappily, ever rising from its initial plane. (Isn't this rather the case of J. Huxley, too?) The author sees the statistical character of human speciation very clearly, as he also sees the irreversibility in the "universalization" of our culture. But he does not seem to have the least suspicion of the fact that human "reflection" ("coreflection") is a

*See page 10.

directed process which points upward, toward a critical point in the Species still ahead. Too faithful to the ideas of "Grandpapa," Charles Darwin does not see the great phenomenon of biological convergence, in Man's case, as anything beyond the fight for life. He simply clings to natural selection.—Books like his give me a longing to push onward *out* of "The Human Phenomenon"....

That's it for today. St. Seine wrote me a fine letter.—Just a little sad between the lines.

> Most affectionately always,
> TEILHARD

Did I tell you the excellent impression made on me by a book which recently came out here (*The Retreat of Christianity from the Modern World* by an Anglican, one Reverend Casserly)? Christianity, he says, is essential to the survival of humanity, but in order to survive, it must "surpass itself." The Reverend Casserly has stolen my word—and what a long time I spent looking for it!

> New York, March 1, 1953

Dear Friend,

... I quite agree with you. Research (the evolutionary act *par excellence*) is destined to become the essential human gesture of tomorrow, and hence, the highest form of "Christification" as well as of adoration.—As a matter of fact, *when seen* from this point of view, "Contemplation" itself becomes a department of research). Under these conditions it seems to me that the essential priestly function right now lies in discovering and realizing in oneself the particular form of interior attitude (passion, audacity, respect, sense of "communion") which most completely satisfies the hearts and minds of the Workers of the Earth, which we are called to be, in the deepest possible way. If we look at all things in this light, the greatest discoveries (in *spiritual* energy of course) can be made in the most humble tasks.

... On my side, there is nothing new—except that I have fallen miserably back into one of my crises of anxiety. (It's more or less like the one I had in 1948, and is quite painful.) Fr. Ravier very intelligently and vigorously told me not to yield to it, but to go on to Africa. . . . I pray that God will fortify me from within. While I wait, I try to maintain what intellectual strength I have. I'm outlining some sketches for my paper on "The Future of the Human Species," and I've written a fairly long letter to J. Huxley in which I insist on the possible difference—a thing which must be verified by facts, as much as it can be—between human "confluence" and human "convergence." As I see it, the former ends by generating a "pool" (Huxley's expression), and the second leaves open the possibility (or rather the probability) of a critical point of reflection (or speciation) *"en avant."*

At Park Avenue, de Breuvery remains my great resource. He seems to be making a place for himself at the United Nations, despite the paradox of his being a Jesuit in a department entirely occupied by non-Christians. In this regard, things are a little tense for him right now. But he has good reasons to be optimistic.

Malvina is busy modeling her "toros" and "toreadors." I telephoned her recently. I did it, in fact, to ask for the address and the aid of her friend Dr. Simard—a splendid man! . . .

In deep affection,
TEILHARD

New York, March 22, 1953

Dear Friend,

My dreadful "nervousness" continued, even though my doctor (Simard, a friend of Carrel as well as Malvina) . . . agrees that I seem better. Still, I pray to God it will subside. The most painful aspect of this problem is the anguish that I feel every time I have to make a decision, or move out of myself in any way.—And the moment when I must be particularly bright and mobile is almost upon me!—Meanwhile, I try to work more or less, and always in the same direction, in my effort to unite "the Human Phenomenon" (defined particularly by its work of coreflection) to general evolution. In today's *New York Times*, Ashley Montague gave an excellent review of Huxley's new book *Evolution in Action.* He pointed out Huxley's tendency to give too much room to the phenomenon of competition as compared with that of "cooperation" in the mechanism of evolution. But by the same token, in this review, Montague himself does not go far enough toward recognizing at what point in Man (because Man is "reflective") this cooperation reaches a form and intensity thus far undreamed of. Thus he ends his review by making Species literally dissolve bit by bit upon itself. Then he concludes: "If man can learn to understand that the greatest of his new qualities is love, then the realization of his evolutionary destiny is assured." This thought could not be better put—short of wondering *how,* outside of an intense "Mystique," the desired unanimity will ever be realized. And to my eyes, the heart of the problem (at the same time that it points the direction for its solution) is precisely this: a meeting between the "Physical" and the "Mystical" in the domain of evolative energetics. . . . But, I repeat, how can one talk about all this without being repudiated by both the "savants" and the Theologians?

. . . Saw Malvina two weeks ago. She has finished her "toros" and "toreadors" and she plans to go to France in May. She's still in great form.—De Breuvery continues to make a place for himself (and not without resistance) at the United Nations. It really seems as though he is going to have the pleasure of making the little clique into which he is fallen jump a bit.

Soon I'll send you the rest of the news.

> In great affection, and in Christ,
> TEILHARD

New York, April 16, 1953

Dear Friend,

    . . . Finally, I really feel I am emerging from my depression of last winter. (It had its clarifying effects, which I'll explain to you one day.) I've started working and talking with people with more ease and pleasure. I dined last week at Malvina's. She's getting ready to go back to Europe. She has finished, had cast in bronze and aluminum, and begun to "position" her four groups of "toros" and "toreadors." They are very (too?) naturalistic, like everything she does, but extraordinarily alive, audacious and clever.—Yesterday they held an official cocktail party (too many people!) at the Alliance Française, to welcome the new cultural attaché, Pierre Donzelot, formerly the Director of Public Education on the Rue de Grenelle, and before that, a director at the Institute of Chemistry at Nancy (or something like that). He did me the honor of telling me that he had a few of my clandestines, which Brandicourt had lent him and which he never returned.—Maritain was there, too (the second time I saw him in ten days), just as humanly sympathetic and, it seems to me, just as incapable of thinking in terms of the dimensions of Cosmogenesis. He can only imagine "changing" Man morally, of course; and he doesn't even seem to suspect that since the time of Aristotle and St. Thomas, Man has changed radically.

    Meanwhile, I continue to pile up sketches and notes with a view toward writing (when?) "The Future of the Human Species." I think the essay is finally taking form. Of course, my objective in writing it is not to "prove," but to "suggest"; and also to let loose a certain number of notions and problems to whose existence (if not solution) it is impossible to shut one's mind from now on.—In this regard, I couldn't restrain myself from writing a fairly long letter to LeBlond* (at Chantilly) on the

---

*Jesuit philosophy specialist, at the moment the "director" of the journal *Etudes.*

subject of his recent article in *Etudes:* "Atheism at the Collège de France." In a very friendly tone, I told him:

1.) that the phenomenology of Husserl, Merleau-Ponty, etc., seems to me to flounder in a pre-Galilean cosmos:

2.) that the Thomist notion of the Absolute Contingency of the Universe (in other words, of God's absolute "liberty" to create or not to create) has the triple and incurable weakness of rendering the Cross absurd, the Pleroma vain, and Work on Man's part in advancing the world in and around him quite insipid.— The farther I go, the less I understand why the leaders of Christianity cannot see how radically disadapted (rather than supremely adaptable) to the *Weltanschauung* is the version of the "Christian vision" they so obstinately defend.—By the way, somebody from the Procure des Missions on the Rue de Grenelle sent me a book called *Regressive Evolution* by a certain Bertrand-Serret. It's a kind of byproduct of the Salet-Lafont book, *The Transformist Superstition.* Naturally I tossed it in the wastebasket; but not before having leafed through it sufficiently to have been shocked before the strict and purely negative obscurantism to which Christianity seems to have degenerated among certain categories of the faithful. It's another case of *Corruptio Optimi Pessima.*

Of course, I must have forgotten at least half the things I wanted to tell you. I'll put them in my next letter.

Affectionately as ever,
TEILHARD

January 26, 1953

Dear Friend,

. . . Thank you for having corrected the proofs . . . to be sent to the *Revue Scientifique,* and thank you for your suggestion on what I wrote apropos mutations. And speaking again of culturation and speciation, I understand your objections better now. I made them to myself, in fact, all this winter, while I was doing the preparatory work on the "Future of the Species." In my present state of mind, however, this is what I think:

1.) *Minimally*, it seems legitimate to me to consider, that in the case of Man (in order to cover the whole biological phenomenon) we must concede the emergence of a new form of speciation, more rapid, more subtle and of a greater capacity and sensibility than the old one, than a speciation based on the accumulation and transmission of a certain trait *acquired*, not in the chromosomes but in what I call the "noosphere" (Huxley's "human pool"). It seems to me incontestable that, through the interplay of socialization and coreflection, a certain *common human fund* of ideas, techniques, aspirations, etc. is constructed little by little, and always more quickly and more tightly. This is in no sense a smaller "common multiple" or a residue, but an organically selected (rather than a statistically selected) extract starting with "individual acquirements" looked at as a whole. To this common fund, newborn individuals accede by education, at the very least.

2.) But is that all there is to it? Or rather, is not the "noospheric" milieu itself capable, in the long run, of acting on the chromosomes of individuals? Or put another way, after a certain number of generations, for example, are not certain perceptions (such as those which evolative Time or that of human convergence—cosmic sense, sense of species, etc.) destined to be inherited directly, outside of education—the way the otter's fishing instinct is?

Actually, I think that there is room here for reworking the relationship between heredity and education. In the case of insects in particular, where instinct (if I'm not mistaken) is admittedly of a hereditary chromosomic nature, it seems to me that only a real gambler would hold that certain behaviorisms (hunting, nest-making, etc.) among adults who never see their parents, are not acquired habits, before being "chromosized." In other words, one absolutely must distinguish between individual *acquired* characteristics which are not there already, and acquired characteristics which are absorbed into the "baggage" of the species.

As far as I can see, the real weak point of present genetics lies in the fact that everything is explained, except the genesis of genes (where the real problem of evolution lies).* The essence of evolution is that it is *additive*, in other words, it accumulates certain acquired traits. Through their fear of falling into a naively finalist Lamarckianism, will not the neo-Darwinists end up by "additivity" (which actually entails suppressing all movement)? Hence this childish tendency of American paleontologists (Simpson, Jepson, etc.) to undervalue the importance of "trends" in phylogenesis by hiding behind the fact of the non-linearity of species. They are like physicists who are afraid of Entropy. (Apropos of this naive Anglo-Saxon neo-Darwinism, last week Grassé wrote me a rough but deeply felt letter.)

Still, while mulling over the "book" I'm thinking of doing, I've recently been led to the question of "the Energy of Evolution" and its two terms:

1.) thermodynamic reserve, etc., and

2.) a psychic drive (or impetus) which is visible at least at the level of man, in other words, with the entrance of self-evolution into the evolutionary system (as I'm always saying, without a passion for peaks in someone like Herzog, there would have been no ascension of Anapurna). But in precisely what the deuce does the relationship (energetically speaking) between physico-chemical "attractions" and "psychic attractions" (or between mechanical work and an effort of will) consist? And how is the linkup made? How is one to define and treat this imponderable and, at the same time, perfectly essential relationship of excitation and activation between Soma and Psyche?

Whatever be the explanations given (I tried years ago in *The Phenomenon of Man* to distinguish between tangential energy [thermo-dynamic energy, etc.] and radial [or psychic] energy,

---

*At just about that time James Watson and Francis Crick published their findings on the structure of DNA, thus revolutionizing the study of genetics.

the result of my present reflections inclines me to reject metaphysics even further. Right now I an inclined to concentrate more and more on Energetics, since Energetics alone is capable of defining the basic conditions which all culture, all morality, and even all religion must satisfy if they are to function.—With this understood, one sees that Christianity can only survive and triumph *when*, through its vision of things, it shows itself capable of activating to the maximum degree, Man's energy of "self-evolution." In other words, if the Church is to *succeed* in the eyes of Man, not only must it "amorize" the World (i.e., teach it to love) more than any religion does, it must also "valorize" it (i.e., teach it to know its own worth). So went my letter to LeBlond. And I've taken the subject up again in six pages on "Contingency and Creation" (or the necessary rethinking of the Thomist theory of "participated being") which I sent confidentially to Fr. Ravier. Yes, the Energetic conditions of religion (with "energetic conditions" having the same relationship to religion as "economico-socio conditions" have to Marxism) seem to me a solid and fruitful base to build on.

Apart from all this, my life goes on as always. I feel decidedly better—nervously, I mean. I'm now at the point where (if nothing happens!) I seriously plan my departure for South Africa. The sailing date of the ship (which goes direct from New York to Cape Town) was just delayed from June 20 to 29 . . . A seventeen-day trip.—The digging subsidized by the W.G. Foundation has just started north of Pretoria.—A little Choukoutien, but probably younger (Old Paleolithic). It's the only strata of this type yet found south of the Sahara.

I plan to return in the beginning of November (via Chile this time, because it's shorter than the Rio route) to see some of the formations of the Pampas and part of the Andes.—

After that, I'll cast a serious glance in the direction of France.

Best of luck in everything.
And in faithful affection,
TEILHARD

LETTERS FROM MY FRIEND TEILHARD

P.S.

It seems that Schante* is still in Peking. If you can get his address from the Procure des Missions, I'll try to write him to find out if he knows anything about our publications. Young told me that nothing is known about them, but he hasn't inquired of Pei.—I think I understand.

New York, May 31, 1953

Dear Friend,

It's Sunday and I write you from Park Avenue without a typewriter. Furthermore this letter will probably cross yours in the mails.—Oh, well!

How are you? . . . As far as I'm concerned on the whole, everything goes well, with the difference that the coming-and-going of summer has just begun. This week Fejos leaves for Europe. And I can feel the time of my own embarkation approaching. Our tickets were booked for a long tour that theoretically will bring me back in the beginning of November via Buenos Aires and Santiago. (I want to see just once the formations of the Pampas and sections of the Andes.) We leave here June 29 direct to Cape Town. Seventeen days, since I won't take the airplane like everybody else! I'll write you again when I get there.

In the interim I continue to scribble. I wrote two essays this month: one (already sent to P. Ravier) on the necessity of rethinking the idea of creation (which, with its brutal metaphysical notion of the *Ens a se* dangerously devaluates "participated being" (by which I mean the created Universe) which the scientific vision tends, on the contrary, to *valorize*. The other essay (which by chance I also sent to Russo) is on "the Energy of Evolution," a rather vague attempt to unravel the energetic relationship between physical (thermodynamic) and psychic (the force

*Pere Louis Schante was a French missionary to China, whose speciality was philosophy. During the time Teilhard was assigned to Chabanel Hall, near Peking, the two men became friends and often discussed philosophy together.

of excitation, activation and attraction) energy in the development of the living being and above all in Man. In fact, it's this "energetic" side of things which more and more tends to take first place in my preoccupations, because it is this reality which is most sure, and the one thing which nothing—not even metaphysics—can ignore.

Incidentally, I was greatly impressed by a strong well written article in the last *Scientific American* in which the results of the first investigations from Mt. Palomar Observatory were exposed. Nothing essentially new there, except that the article made it apparent that the distances that we imagined existed in and between galaxies must at least be doubled. This simple reaffirmation made me feel even more sharply the absurdity of the position (too evident, alas, in the recent volume of "Recherches et Debats" published by the "Intellectuelles Catholiques," which says that Christianity remains unchanged *whatever* the appearance our experience gives us of the size, structure and organicity of the Universe.—This religious "isolationism" is just as destructive as the "concordism," which (with good reason) we wish to avoid. There is a resonance between adoration and science—and there must be a coherence. To take a crude example, how is it that church people still claim not to understand how much man's view of his world has changed, given: 1) that life is a natural prolongation of atomization and molecularization; 2.) that reflection is a natural prolongation of consciousness; and 3) that there are millions of galaxies where the same physical, chemical reactions as are found in the Milky Way are going on?

How, I repeat, is it that they cannot see that under these conditions, the "plurality of inhabited worlds has once and for all ceased to be an imagination *à la Fontenelle,** and that from now on it is a "greater probability" which the Christian *Weltanschauung* must satisfy. (All this without rushing to the unthinkable escape hatches of "galaxies which are not affected by

*Bernard La Bouvier de Fontenelle (1657–1751). French man of letters, author (1686) of "Entretien sur la Pluralité des Mondes" an attempt to popularize a new astronomical theory. M.L.

original sin (!!), or a *terrestrial* redemption affecting all the galaxies!!!) On this point, as on many others (eugenics, for example) the Theologians are serenely sitting on the top of a volcano or over an abyss which they do not see, because they refuse to admit that two and two make four (even in those favorable cases where they are capable of counting up to two, or in other words, of measuring the isolated evidence of these three points).—I'm completely done with Theologians!—Still, I become furious when I see them maintain Christianity in so stunted a form that the Gentiles (to say nothing of many Christians) are disgusted by it. Since Christianity is fundamentally the only "religious" phylum capable of amorizing the universe, from the simple point of view of energetics, it must do this at any price so that hominization may continue—Again I ask, why is it that in Rome, along with a "Biblical Commission" there is no "Scientific Commission" charged with pointing out to authorities the points on which one can be sure Humanity will take a stand tomorrow—points, I repeat, such as: 1.) the question of eugenics (aimed at the optimum rather than the maximum in reproduction, and joined to a gradual separation of sexuality from reproduction); and 2.) the absolute right (which must, of course, be regulated in its "timing" and its conditions!) to try everything right to the end—even in the matter of human biology; and 3.) the admitted existence (because statistically it's more probable) of Foyers of Thought in every galaxy. All this descends directly on us—for general reasons of universal order and for basic reasons. And while all this is going on churchmen really think that they can still satisfy the world by promenading a statue of Fatima across the continents!—This kind of thinking manifests itself here in New York too, where Catholic organizations are noisily separating themselves from Trusts or Boards of charitable organizations which have agreed to associate with groups interested in methods of eugenics (even though these groups are just as interested in fecundity as they are in birth prevention).—O Pharisees! . . .

I don't know why I'm telling you all this. It's without any

bitterness, really. ("They" are already done for, and they know it!) Doubtless I'm going because it's Sunday and the morning is long. And also because so much leads to reflection of this kind ever since the nostalgic childishness of the [Presidential] Coronation led to internecine schism among the Republicans in Washington. Everywhere, the signs that the world must shed (and is in the process of shedding) its old skin are now present.—But under what sign will it make a new skin? It's here that the question of rethinking the Meaning of the Sign of the Cross becomes important.

Most affectionately,
TEILHARD

New York, June 15, 1953

Dear Friend,

Thank you for Schanté's address. Of course, I'll try to pass it on to Young so that he too can try 1.) to find out where our publications are; and 2.) to see that they are passed on to the Geological Survey where at least they will be safe and utilized.

Meanwhile, there's nothing new, except that my departure time approaches. The sailing has been delayed from June 29 to July 1, now.—I'm not particularly enthusiastic about this type of work which seems less and less "vital" to me. All the same, I am aware that at the present moment I may be able to give a useful lift to the researchers themselves in the organization of their labor, and also, as I told you, because I need this humble platform to make myself listened to.—Just as it was two years ago, Johannesburg will be my point of departure, but perhaps I will be able to push on to Rhodesia this time; I would like to see certain deposits there.—After July 1 write me at the Langham Hotel, Johannesburg, South Africa, where I expect to arrive on July 25th. I'm counting very much on these months to give me a new start on life and to provide me with ideas about Man, about the continents, and also (if not above all) about the present state and future of "hominization."

As to this last matter (as to its logical connection, "Christianization," if I dare say it) I feel my thought concentrating more and more around a small number of precise and, I think, penetrating axes. All this has had as its result a closer and closer tie for me with the Church," and a loosening more and more of my ties with "church people." Did I tell you how disappointed I was recently when I read an article ("Problems and the Mystery of Human Progress") in the *Nouvelle Revue Théologique*, which my friend R. very kindly sent me? It's difficult to imagine a more half-baked, slippery mélange of the new spirit and of prehistoric theology than is found there. Not the slightest realization or vision of the Human Phenomenon! Still, at the base of the universe, the good old "mystery of iniquity." And still the good old "supernatural," so monstrously isolated from all biology! I very politely wrote Russo what I think about it.—I wouldn't be surprised if (as he wrote me) he did not let the whole thing loose when he spoke at Versailles on Ascension Day.

Along the same line of ideas, I have just finished writing (and sending to Fr. Ravier) a near-treatise—well, six pages anyway—on the present prolongations of the human theological problems arising from the current scientific recognition of the possibility of a plurality of "inhabited worlds." Given what we now know about:

1.) The emergence (through the play of more or less preferential chance) of life from chemicals and Reflectivity from living beings; and

2.) The immense number of galaxies whose chemistry is obviously the same as in our own Milky Way.

Under such conditions, the *probability* of numerous centers of psychic Reflection in the Universe with at least one Earth per galaxy (in other words, millions of them) is much greater than the contrary possibility. How can we then continue to teach (as a dogmatically "sure thing") a geocentric (or "monogeocist"*) Christianity which once and for all has become astronomically improbable, just as for over a century it's been impossible to insist on strict monogenism (descent from only one couple).

As I wrote to Ravier, this note is the fourth piece of a dossier which I hope he will one day pass on to whoever handles things like this, so that at last at Rome they'll understand that, in the present century, it is inevitable that mankind take a position on a series of questions which the Theologians still refuse even to consider.—Among the other pieces I plan for the dossier are: 1.) the duty of facing up to problems in Eugenics, and the 2.) Right to Research.—If Christianity does not take the lead in meeting all these points head on, a new *Weltanschauung* and a new Morality will be constructed without us.—Perhaps the world will die because of this. But so will we.

There's very little news to give you. Fejos is in Europe; Malvina is in Paris; and on the 24th de Breuvery will fly to Paris *(Etudes)* for a month as well. Try not to miss him.

As you can see by this scribbling, it's Sunday again and I'm at St. Ignatius on Park Avenue.

I won't say anything about the political scene here. You know as much as I do. As for the details, de Breuvery can fill you in.

In great affection as ever,
TEILHARD

P.S.

As I reread this letter, I say . . . Yes. There are two demons (among others) to be exorcised from Christianity:

the demon of mono*gen*esis
and
the demon of mono*geo*cism.

---

*Relating to only *one* planet: earth. (From the Greek root "Geo".)

LETTERS FROM MY FRIEND TEILHARD

Purchase (N.Y.) June 26, 1953

Dear Friend,

... I received your letter written on the 23rd—which gave
me great pleasure because it made me feel we understand each
other better and better,—not only in terms of human affection,
but in "the ever greater Christ," Who is the most solid and dynamic bond of friendship...."
... I'm writing you from the country house of the Strauses
(Guggenheim).... In other words, the delightful place where I
have already spent a week last year before going to California—
Flowers, deep green, and absolute calm. This rest before going
on my voyage is particularly good.... Finally after so many de-
lays and longshoremen's strike (four days only, happily), *The African Endeavour* is supposed to weigh anchor on July 1st from
Brooklyn.—Seventeen days out of sight of land is a bit long. But
the crossing is said to be agreeable and (judging from the price
of the ticket!) it should be extremely comfortable.—As usual,
I'm thinking of writing something on board. But I still hesitate
between two subjects. Should I begin my "book" (?) on "the sin-
gularity (the singularities?) of the Human Species" or should I
instead (in a few unpublishable pages) on the two principal axes
which have become "the real Goal and real Base" of my kind of
adoration? In any case, two letters recently received from South
Africa prove that down there there will really be something that
I can do—something in the order of a modest supervision, and
of giving fresh impulse to the work. And I am expected.

In deep friendship as ever,
TEILHARD

*By mid-year Teilhard was feeling better. He left New York
on June 29 for a seventeen-day voyage. He used the time on*

176

shipboard to write "The Convergence of the Universe," an essay in which he once more fixed the principal axis of what had become his form of adoration, and to make notes for a second text called the "Singularities of the Human Species," in which he would examine his most recently developed views on the subject.

When he arrived in Africa, he stopped at Cape Town to examine some particularly new Neanderthal fossils dug up from the dunes of Hopefield. Then he went on to Johannesburg, and to Pretoria to meet J.T. Robinson, head of the Museum there. Next he traveled 300 kilometers north to see the great dig at Makapan, site of the Australopithecine deposits. In South Africa he opted for an "interruption" between men and Australopithecines rather than a direct descent. In other words, Teilhard did not see a direct filiation between the two neighboring forms. Facing these problems, and encouraged by the ardor of the young researchers on the spot, he dreamed of forming an international team in Africa to study the whole continent South of the Sahara to Cape Town in view of better defining and better comprehending the origins of man. As the venture ended, he felt renewed.

Hotel Langham, Johannesburg
August 5, 1953

Dear Friend,

... With some astonishment and much pleasure I find myself in a country which after 1951, I thought I'd never see again, and which today I feel as though I'd never left. We even have the same hotel rooms which we had two years ago! The sea voyage down here was quite agreeable. After seventeen days on the water, without seeing anything except Ascension Island and St.

LETTERS FROM MY FRIEND TEILHARD

Helena, under almost continuously clear skies, our comfortable little ship (10,000 tons) arrived at Cape Town to find pure spring weather. (Just a week ago, there was a fairly uncomfortable cold wave. Nor is it quite gone.)—We stayed ten days at Cape Town, just long enough to see a very Neanderthaloid brain-pan, unearthed this year in the solidified fossiliferous dunes of Hopefield, and to discuss the continuation of the operations there.— Right afterward we came up here to Johannesburg, where I have already accomplished quite a lot. I visited Pretoria to see Robinson and the new Australopithecine material, and more recently went to see the great digs at Makapan (three hundred kilometers to the north of here, on the asphalt road that goes from the Cape to Cairo), where my friend van Riet-lowe (with the financial aid of the W.G. Foundation) is in the process of clearing a "little Choukoutien." On the whole, I'm very interested by everything I see—whether it be from the general point of view of human origins—or from the particular point of view of deepening the stratigraphy which should be followed to mount a general attack on Africa south of the Sahara. With a good five-year plan (to which I hope to convert Fejos), it seems possible to establish at Makapan a dig of several different layers, one atop the other, going from the Australopithecine (Lower Pleistocene beds) all the way up to and including the Upper Paleolithic. With this and two or three other similar points (among them, Hopefield near Cape Town and Olduvai Gorge in Tanganyika) a first triangulation could be achieved south of the Sahara. To complete the network, I hope, toward the beginning of September, to go to Lusaka in Northern Rhodesia where they have just found some breccias of a Pre-Chellian appearance. All this organizational work is much more intriguing in that, thanks to Fejos' friendship, I really feel I am touching the "nerve" of the battle. What's more, I can see a vigorous and winning team of young people developing on the job—an international team, very like the one which made the research into Early Man in the Far East so fascinating before 1939—but this time here in Africa.

I am also profoundly interested by the economic and social condition of this country, where, in a land still peopled by cattledrivers, a uranium industry is developing at an implacable and ever-accelerating pace. On the other hand, I still feel the savagery of this countryside from which the great animals have (unhappily and inevitably) disappeared over the last 70 years. (Imagine, elephants and giraffes still walked around Pretoria when I was born!)—Everything is grayer or more yellow this month, but just the same, the aloes are in bloom, and red, pink or yellow flowers appear everywhere among the umbrella-like acacias and the candelabra-like euphorbia, brightening the view. —I'm speaking now about the brush north of Pretoria which extends all the way to Abyssinia. Around Johannesburg, on this high plateau, the spectacle is more austere; but the light in this season is magnificent. An imperturbably blue sky, weather gray and crisp—exactly like Peking toward the end of autumn. There's a little frost in the morning . . .

> Most affectionately always,
> TEILHARD

> Hotel Langham, Johannesburg
> September 9, 1953

Dear Friend,

. . . Here, since the fifth of August things continue to develop favorably. The high point of our stay so far has been a trip at the end of August to Northern Rhodesia, where I went to the Lusaka region to see a series of fissures containing fossiliferous breccias and tool-like objects which perhaps will establish a bridge between the Australopithecine beds and the first African pebble industry. I hope to convince the W.G. Foundation to underwrite a dig there which just might act as an important point in the "triangularization" of human origins south of the Sahara.

LETTERS FROM MY FRIEND TEILHARD

In the course of this circuit, I learned a great deal. But I also saw a most impressive landscape whose appearance has not changed since Livingstone's time.—Immense undulating surfaces covered with deep brush, or, at the end, now that we're approaching the dry season, a certain number of trees beginning to green at the base of great yellow plants.—Up river, Victoria Falls (where I spent two days) one can still easily see the hippopotami, peacefully bathing in the Zambezi.—From Jo-burg to Livingstone, we traveled in a Comet jet (less than two hours, instead of three days on the railroad or in a car coming and going, but following a trajectory which reaches some 12,000 meters at its height and does not permit one to see very much). On the return trip, however, with good light, I could clearly recognize a great salt pan in the Kalahari.

And now I'm spending my last days at Jo-burg. Tomorrow I must return to Pretoria, to the Geologic Service and to Robinson, then the following week I plan on looking at the great digs at Makapan again before they are started again next year. As I told you, it's a question of establishing here a complete series joining the Australopithecine beds with the bifaced tools. No human remains have been found here yet, which is a small disappointment. But the best part of the deposit has perhaps not yet been approached.—On the whole, I will leave here satisfied, entirely convinced that the enterprise is well begun and that it's only a question of "sprinkling" a few more digs at 6 or 7 good spots, going from the Cape to Tanganyika.—The thing I missed (because I didn't know how to go there without taking a yellow fever shot) is not having seen the magnificent lacustrine series in the Great Lakes region. It's too bad, really.

We leave Johannesburg on September 20th and embark from Cape Town around the 27th for Buenos Aires. Until the 26th you can write me a letter at the Mount Nelson Hotel in Cape Town.

Otherwise there's nothing new. De Breuvery must be really worn out in New York; he sends me no news of the common possibility of our staying next year at St. Ignatius (Park Avenue) where, when I left, they were planning to remodel. From France I received an excellent letter from Ravier (my provincial at Lyon) telling me about the nomination of my young and brilliant friend, Jacques Sommet* as rector of Fourvière.—A master stroke, it seems to me! Is it possible that things are clearing up on the Roman hills?

... In faithful and deep affection, as ever,

TEILHARD

Teilhard left Johannesburg on September 20 for Cape Town and Cape Town on the 27th for Argentina. From this last lap of his voyage he had not perhaps gotten everything that he wanted. He had planned to see Chile and part of the Andes, but a series of unforeseen circumstances obliged him to change his itinerary drastically. He did, however, manage to drop in on the German anthropologist Menghin again, to examine the latest work on prehistoric man in Patagonia. His trip to Africa pleased him greatly. He felt in better health than he had in a long time. He was satisfied with the plan he had set up for the triangularization of the study of the remains of fossil man south of the Sahara, and he had in hand six notes and articles.

The future of man continued to occupy him. He turned his attention to the question of the "Activation of Human Energy" for which he had given the outline in the Revue des Questions Scientifiques. *It was not essentially the cry of alarm which came from those who feared dying of hunger in an overpopulated world that worried him, nor the protests of those who feared the problems created by over-industrialization. What troubled him most of all was the more fundamental thought that those who had the world in their keeping (in other words, us, the human race) might lose heart for the human adventure itself. This idea necessarily led him back to a description of the Divine Motor*

---

*Jesuit theology professor from Chantilly, one-time French Catholic Resistance hero, deported to Dachau by the Germans.

*which sustained the thirst for life. To his Provincial he wrote a
note on "The God of Evolution," telling how, as he conceived it,
God should be made present in all activities and techniques.*

On Board
SS Argentina, October 21, 1953

Dear Friend,

This letter, mailed tonight at Rio, is to tell you that right
now I am sailing on back north. I'm due in New York on November 2nd. I hope to have a letter from you waiting for me at
the W.G. Foundation. It seems centuries to me since we wrote
to each other.

As it turned out, I had to shorten my return-trip plans. Arrived in Buenos Aires (on the *Tjisedame*, a little Dutch tramp
steamer which once (in 1936) took me from Batavia to Shanghai
and which has now ambitiously taken on the route from Tokyo
to South America. All the staff were Chinese "boys": Wang,
Chang, etc.) When we docked at Buenos Aires, after 18 days of
seeing nothing but gray sky and albatrosses, we found out that
the railroad line to Valparaiso had been cut in the Andes, and
that our Grace Line steamer could not move as a result of a
dockers' strike. Therefore, we decided to make a shift to the
Moore-McCormack Line (an ultra-Catholic company where I
get a discount because I am a priest.—I really don't like that sort
of thing). It will be a bit monotonous; I already know the route.
But it's the wise decision.—So I will not see the Pampas, nor the
Andes, nor Guayaquil. Too bad, really.—In Buenos Aires with
Dr. Menghin I inspected the most recent results of the research
on Early Man in Patagonia, a collection simultaneously disap-
pointing and curious, representing the end of the voyage toward
Cape Horn of that great Paleolithic wave 6,000 years ago, which
started in Africa some hundreds of thousands of years earlier. So
I have not absolutely wasted my time and money here.

As I wrote from Jo-burg, I'm coming back satisfied. I hope I can make my case to Fejos, and that he understands and will accept the fine strategy so manifestly needed in Africa.—And then, I'm returning with several ideas for work to do: 1.) a communication (already written) for the Academy on the opportunity to distinguish two distinct centers of hominzation in the Lower Pleistocene: the principal one in Africa; the other (which aborted before reaching the level of "Sapiens") in Indonesia; 2.) a project for an article, aimed at the *Revue des Questions Scientifiques* (?) on "the Activation of Human Energy"; 3.) a project for a note (for Ravier and the initiated) on "The God of Evolution"; 4.) an article for Piveteau *(Annales de Paléontologie)* on the Figures (Patterns) of Speciation; and 5.) finally, and this is just a thought, an article for Vaufrey *(L'Anthropologie)* on the present state of research on the origins of Man in Africa.

I really don't know when I'll finish all this.

I'll write you in the beginning of November from New York to tell you the situation there. I hope that dear Father Gannon will find me a corner at Park Avenue with de Breuvery again.—Incidentally, I have not heard a word from him.

Affectionately,
TEILHARD

Since the rector of St. Ignatius had announced his intention of completely remodeling the place, Teilhard had not been sure of where he would be living when he returned to New York. Happily, though, for the moment at least, his "little room at Park Avenue" was still there. His desk was full of letters and documents. Rest after travel is often enervating. But in this case, nothing slowed down the returnee's intellectual activity. The projects he had contemplated during the October trip took shape. The note to the Academy was in the mail, and he was thinking of writing two more little para-scientific studies.

Teilhard's letter of November 9, 1953, brought good news. At last, he wrote me he felt sure he would be able to come back briefly to Paris. I was overjoyed, to say the least.

LETTERS FROM MY FRIEND TEILHARD

But what neither of us knew was that this trip of 1954 would be the last time he would leave America.

New York, November 9, 1953

Dear Friend,

. . . Would you believe last Sunday, in the Public Gardens in Philadelphia a crowd (with prayers, sick people, candles, and some $1,500 left as offerings on the ground) gathered in the hope of seeing the reappearance of a "Lady in Blue and White" glimpsed (?) by two little girls in the beginning of the month? Nothing happened. And the Archbishop let it be known that he had no comment. Still the same old Lourdes-Fatima contagion! Is this sort of thing a residual "craving" for the marvelous? Or, on the contrary, should it be seen as a popular symptom of the growing impossibility for a humanity in the process of (and on the path of) growing reflectivity to live any longer in a "closed Universe"?—to live, in other words, in a universe that has no answer to the "pull" which comes from "Beyond"?—Never have I felt so strongly this (inevitable) drama of Thought awakening in the Night!—Nor have I ever felt so strongly that people have a need—and by this I don't mean wishful thinking but a biological need for "Revelation," provided it can be stated in a fashion compatible with what we are beginning to glimpse of the laws of "Noogenesis," and not as a function of a henceforth inacceptable conception of the miraculous and supernatural.

As for me, I've moved back into my office in the W.G. Foundation and have even found my little room on Park Avenue—a thing I'm happy about (de Breuvery hasn't changed at all). I've quite a few things to do and to straighten out during these first days, of course. I sent a communication to the Academie on the probability of two subcenters of "human evolution": the one aborted in Indonesia; the other, the principal one, in Africa; and I finished transcribing my piece for Vaufrey's *L'Anth-*

184

*ropologie.** After that, I'm going to work on two little parascientific studies (for the use of Ravier and Sommet), the more interesting of which is entitled "God of Evolution."—Otherwise my future is pretty vague, except that I've decided (if I am allowed) to spend three months next year in France: probably June, July and August. Does this mean another game of hide-and-seek? I hope not . . .

Incidentally if you put off your own trip to America a little bit next year, perhaps we can come back together. That way we would see each other twice, in Paris in June and in New York in the autumn. . . .

Yours in Christ,
TEILHARD

New York, December 17, 1953

Dear Friend,

. . . Here I am just in time to send you my most affectionate wishes for Christmas and the New Year, and to wish peace and fire (simultaneously) in your heart. This is the thing I pray for you as I pray for it for myself.

For three months now, there has really been nothing new in my life. After having put down a certain number of papers which I had in mind (or even wrote during the crossing) for the Academie, for Vaufrey's *L'Anthropologie,* and even for Lyon (a Note on "The God of Evolution"!), I set myself to thoughtfully write a little book (?) on Man which will be called *The Singularities of the Human Species.* Of course, it will still press home the old ideas, but as I always hope, do it in a slightly better "focused" and more publishable form. The most recent spur to my hesitations in starting it (I've had the notes on the subject together for a year) comes from J. Rostand's new book, *Ce Que Je Crois.* That

---

*Vaufrey, Raymond. Prehistorian, then Professor at the Institute of Human Paleontology in Paris.

avowal is a very touching and a very poor piece at the same time. In terms of paleontologic insight, it goes no further than Vialleton. And what can I say about its portrayal of the miserable mission of the formidable "Human Phenomenon!"—After reading it, plus Charles Galton-Darwin and even Huxley (that makes three times in one year that professional biologists have undervalued the Human), it seems the time has come, even from the scientific point of view, to show that it's possible to read the same facts quite differently and more convincingly. . . .

. . . De Breuvery continues to navigate the troubled and troubling waters of UNO without sinking. I'm happy to know he's under the same roof with me.

I have to end this letter from Park Avenue a bit brusquely. Write me quickly. And again, Happy New Year.

Most affectionately,
TEILHARD

1954

Teilhard in the Luxembourg Gardens, Paris

From a twofold point of view, 1954 was an exceptional year. Teilhard tried to strengthen his position in America, and he made a visit home.

In the first matter, the steps he had to take were difficult. As a result of X-ray examinations which gave a troubling account of the state of his lungs, American immigration authorities hesitated to give him a permanent visa. It was a complication that neither he nor anyone else had expected. He was obliged to argue and call on influential friends for help. But despite the thousand and one services they rendered him, the problem persisted, first in New York and then in Paris.

In other areas, too, most things went badly. In the letters he wrote that, year, Teilhard seems less exuberant, less enthusiastic than usual. Although he tried to keep a cheerful face, inner pessimism and worry affected him physically.

In the early part of the year, he was much preoccupied reading the religio-scientific books that had been sent him by friends in Paris. For example, Jean Rostand had just published his Ce que je crois. With sympathy, Teilhard recognized it was not faith that Rostand lacked "but what really came down to the same thing, simple vision." And in a letter to me, he added, "The title of Rostand's book should be Ce Que Je Ne Crois Pas.

189

LETTERS FROM MY FRIEND TEILHARD

It was a title suggested to him by the daughter of a friend, herself a non-Christian.

In the small collection of letters that follows, there is one fact which we can be sure caused Teilhard pain. To this day no one in France has forgotten the effort that some priests made to evangelize the apparently areligious working class. Cardinal Suhard, Archbishop of Paris, had authorized a small number of them to become workers themselves, to share the work of the poor and be part of their life as witnesses to Christ. But under these circumstances, and in a capitalist world, how does one remain a Christian? It was a burning question. Very sincere attempts were made by ardent and generous priests to adopt that way of life—the same working conditions, the same salary, the same allegiance to the unions as the poor. In such a situation, certain abuses were bound to occur and Church authorities reacted. The Jesuit Father General took the serious step of revoking the permission he had given to members of the Order to continue that apostolate, little dreaming that lack of proper training might be the real cause of the problem. In any case the unhappy end of the worker-priest movement in no way diminishes the nobility of the effort.

Another event that interested Teilhard that year was that, surprisingly enough, in his Christmas message of 1953, Pope Pius XII recognized the value of science and technology, even though he warned Christians against the dangers hidden in the "materialism" thus engendered. The technological mind, he quite properly wrote, must cling to its sense of high value of human life, whenever it tries to exploit the forces and elements of nature. "All research and discovery is basically only the research and discovery of the grandeur and harmony of God," he said. "And if we see it in this light, who can disprove or condemn science . . ."

Was something changing in high places? Teilhard was not convinced. Caught off guard by the Pope's statement, he had himself been so often touched by unjust decisions, that he could *scarcely believe it. On closer examination he saw in the reflections of the pontiff only concessions and no real enthusiasm. It goes without saying that Christians should always be warned against excesses. But what I am sure Teilhard would have preferred to hear from the Pope was an affirmation of the positive value of science in the spiritual life and praise for its role in the completion of a universe still in formation, as it moved toward the ultimate attainment of Christ, its supreme Attraction.*

Once more the Teilhardian faith was in advance of its times. He well knew—he had demonstrated it in his life and writings—that science, such as it is, cannot completely satisfy the needs of Man and that something is necessary. His conclusion was that the human heart could rest only in a twofold love: the love of the World, and the love of Christ.

In this connection, another problem preoccupied Teilhard. What, he asked himself, is the place of the priest? How can Man legitimize his action in so apparently profane a realm? This was not a new preoccupation for Teilhard. Ever since World War I, he had abandoned the life usually followed by priests in order to thrust the great part of his energy into the arid ground of science.

For a long time, he had mourned over the lack of interest of Christians in the affairs of the world that made them regarded by non-Christians as "half brothers" or "false brothers." As he saw it, this state of affairs could not continue. There is no break between the demands of the world and what religion teaches. True Christianity calls on all its adherents to participate in the painful, difficult task of edifying the universe. The place of Man ("body-soul") is the Earth. The goal of his efforts is the Christ Universal.

In such a context, the priest devoted to the sciences is not an intruder into a world for which he is not made; his sacerdotal consecration only brings him a greater sense of human duty. He does not dehumanize the world under the pretext it is full of perversity. If he is to give back to the practice of the Gospels an élan which it should never have lost, he is by nature at war with Manichean pessimism, with Jansenism, with every kind of dualism.

Not everyone accepts these ideas. It should, however, be remembered that they evolve from a philosophy in accordance with the teaching of St. Paul and St. John.

In February 1954, Teilhard received confirmation of the permission he had been promised to return to France for a while. Since I was planning to go to America the following September, we tried to make our plans together. In early June he sailed for France, where he planned to remain for three months.

New York, January 5, 1954

Dear Friend,

. . . I've booked passage for France on the *Flanders* for June 4th with a return ticket on the same boat in first class for September 17. Would it be convenient for you to join me on your own trip to America at that time? In case it would, I'm sending you the card of a travel agent I'm using. . . . How pleasant it would be if you could travel back with me! . . . Otherwise there is nothing at all new here. I'm absorbed in writing an essay, which as a matter of fact I don't even think will turn into a ten-page manuscript. I have the feeling I may also write something on "The Singularities of the Christian Faith"* (considered in its relationship to the activation of human energy) to put in the appendix. Paradoxically, it's probably this very appendix that the censors will make me suppress. Our directors are incorrigible!

I was, of course, deeply pained to hear of the death of Auguste Valensin. No matter how different we were at heart (for him, thought was fundamentally more a game than a life), I am enormously indebted to him. He was a confidant in whose judg-

---

*"Les Singularités de l'Espèce Humaine."

ment one could place implicit trust. And a man of enormous influence on the awakening of religious thought in our time. — Now what does he "see"? I wonder. —And when will my turn come? . . .

Affectionately,
TEILHARD

February 9, 1954

Dear Friend,

I'm following with interest and sympathy the "reincarnations" of your article on the priest in the laboratory. . . . And I agree with you. After all, it is admitted that a researcher may be enlivened in his research by his "communism." Why not then by his Christianity? The fault may lie directly in the "dehumanization" of present-day Christianity, of dehumanization born of false detachment, which makes us appear to "laymen" as demibrothers, if not (unless there is proof to the contrary) as false brothers. As a matter of fact, your article cannot go to the heart of the question without posing again the entire problem of what a priest is (in other words, what a saint is, or to go one step further, what spirit is). It's our notion of Spirituality and Sanctity which is in the process of irresistible change not only among us, but among all men, as they acknowledge the new vision of the universe, which is not drawn in *cosmic,* but in cosmo*genetic* terms.—Still my same old song.—Certainly, as I wrote to Russo the other day, if the priest-workers catch fire from Marxism, it is because they find in the face of a humane Marxism not only justice, but "hope" and a Feeling for the Earth which is stronger than "evangelical humanity"—at least in the form they learned it. Evidently Mauriac does not understand, nor, given his Manichean pessimism, is it possible for him to understand the problem.

. . . For the rest, there's nothing new. Saw a few interesting compatriots, among them, Malraux (whom I met two weeks ago at dinner). I think we understood each other very well.—And, even more easily, thanks to the fact that he knew some of my papers. I rather felt that he really had (as "Onimus," the *Etudes* writer recently said) gone beyond Art, and is trying to discover his own God.—As for the rest, I continue to work on what could turn out to be a little book.—The weather's been a little chilly here.—I'm starting to dream about dogwood in flower and spring. . . .

> In deep affection,
> Yours,
> TEILHARD

New York, March 7, 1954

Dear Friend,

Thank you for your letter of February 12 which I am so late in answering. These last few weeks have been a little busy for me, first of all because I had to spend a few days in Washington, and then because last week I had to search for a place to live outside of St. Ignatius. A problem in the rebuilding there, and arguments with recalcitrant landlords, have forced the charming Father Gannon to put seven Fathers of the house out in the street for three months. And all in eight days. Thanks to the broad-mindedness of Fr. McMahon (the Provincial here), however, and with the aid of Roger Straus, I was able to find a relatively economical asylum in a very chic and quiet men's club (rigorously cloistered!), the Lotos Club, 5 East 66th Street, a few steps from the Wenner-Gren Foundation. It's in a Dominican parish (five minutes by foot to get to the church). So all's well that ends well. But all this moving about neither facilitates my work nor calms my nerves. The latter are pretty ragged at the moment. Patience. I just must be able to establish myself a little better in the "milieu divin."

Naturally, I followed with sharp interest the recent problems of the Dominicans in France.* More and more it seems to me that the problem from now on is irrevocably closed in the live reality of fact: "From now on what should a priest *be*, in order to *remain a priest* in a world where the very notion of spirit is in the process of changing?"

Since over the years, I have put this question in everything I thought or wrote; I consider it a sort of a victory that from now on—despite all constraints—the Church finds itself forced to rethink its system of spiritual values and the whole theory of its "amorization" of the Universe in X. Jesu . . .

. . . After the loss of dear Auguste Valensin, that of Pierre Charles has left me feeling quite abandoned. I think that he (Charles) did change his attitude incredibly since 1946. (But Charles a conservative!?) Still, he remained faithfully attached to me. And he (with Valensin, of course) is one of the two people who opened my eyes long ago when we were studying theology together. One more loss. And when will my turn come?

My little book on Man continues to grow quietly despite everything. . . . Isn't it true that the real excitement lies in discovering the divine at the common heart of everything which is a bit more true and more universal?

In faithful affection,
TEILHARD

New York, March 16, 1954

Dear Friend,

Apropos your article on the priest in the laboratory:

I do not see your problem as fundamentally treatable except as a corollary of a general theory of the reciprocal relationship between Christ and evolution—in other words, as a general theory of Christogenesis (or of the relationship between Spirit and

*In February 1954 the Dominican Master General, Emanuel Suarez, recalled his own men from the priest-worker movement. At the same time he demanded the resignation of three provincials and took steps to reduce the influence of the thought of the theologians Marie-Dominique Chenu and Yves Congar.

Matter, which comes to the same thing). The fullness of Christ is only comprehensible in a universe in convergent evolution (i.e., in a centered universe. And evolution can only achieve itself by "amorization" through Christ incarnate. But with the present prejudices of a theology which is attached to an impossible "Supernatural," and not an ultra (which would be viable), but an *extra* or *para*-evolative meaning. How can one teach that the Eucharistic consecration has a natural meaning which extends to the whole of Cosmogenesis—a teaching which demands that the priest (or the lay quasi-priest) should be everywhere? In sum, the battle over the spiritual value of Matter has already been joined. And I'm persuaded that it's precisely on this point of the capacity of a well-understood Christianity to present Matter as simultaneously Christifying and Christifiable, that the religion of tomorrow will hang.

In passing, I note the following objections:

1.) "Such an ethic is atheistic."—To this I would say no. It is the ethic of the dark adoration of the God before us (cf. the article in *l'Espirit* by LaCroix);

2.) "The priest in the laboratory is not a normal thing."—I would reply that it is normal, because everything is Christifiable and *christicandum*. It is only that we are not yet used to priests in laboratories. That's all.

3.) "Matter is neither good nor bad."—My answer is that Matter is preferentially good, and that in any case it is certainly necessary to the genesis of spirit. "Materia Matrix."—When will theologians understand that Matter and Spirit are not two opposite or simply juxtaposed things, but positively and even genetically joined? . . .

Nothing new here. I'm getting used to my new regime. I continue to write my "opuscule" without being too sure that it will be worth anything when it is finished.—The other day at a cocktail party I ran into Fr. D'Arcy (who preached the Lenten sermons here) and Denis de Rougement.

Most affectionately,
TEILHARD

196

New York, March 30, 1954

Dear Friend,

... What I hear about the reactions to the recently published article on the priest in the laboratory convinces me that the cause of the present barrier to any kind of renaissance and humanization of Christianity is that monstrous "Supernatural" employed by theologians since Augustine. This supernatural was manufactured to explain, in the fixist perspectives we have still not abandoned that Man, because of Adam, found himself *non vulneratus* but at the same time, *spoliatus.* An *extra*-natural, much more than a true *super*-natural—a doctrine which depends on "gratuity," while the beauty and grandeur of all union (properly defined) lies basically in its "necessity!"

What we need right now in order "to adore in spirit and in truth" is quite simply (it seems to me) to recognize that the final coming to its goal, through a critical point, of the general movement of the "Noogenesis" (in which Cosmogenesis, as it now appears to us, consists), is the real "Supernatural."—A Universe, in other words, which, through the final metamorphosis of the Human, rejoins a central and ultrapersonal Foyer of Consciousness. There is nothing else than this in the gospels, or in the mysticism of the saints. (Meanwhile, there is not a grain of spiritual dynamism in the idea of this "ultragratuity" of the Divine, as the Theologians describe it.) In this light, then—or, if you like, if one admits that the Divinization (or rather, the "Christification") of the world begins from the first stages of its arrangement—then everything in Cosmogenesis (everything, in a large but literal sense) becomes the business of consecration—the business of the priesthood. In the present ecclesiastical social structure, one reserves the name of "priest" for those who "consecrate" the world in the last and the supreme degree (whatever all that means). But in *all* evolvative work, there is something to consecrate. And inasmuch as "lay people" have not understood the degree to which they are true priests, it is very necessary that we give the example and take charge of the operation.

197

LETTERS FROM MY FRIEND TEILHARD

You asked me for texts to support this point of view. The text I choose is the word of Christ: "I come not to destroy but to fulfill." *Non veni solvere sed ad implere.* The Christique was not realized to diminish, but to complete "Evolution." As long as our leaders do not understand this, Christianity will remain under-humanized and underhumanizing. And it will not rise from its present sad condition of being (however much people may deny it) a religion for the use of "the underdeveloped." Just the opposite of what it could be, if only it would embrace Evolution. By embracing Evolution in order to save it, the Christian message would be reincarnated and be saved by Evolution.

. . . To you in very great affection,

TEILHARD

New York, Easter 1954

Dear Friend,

This is to send you a brotherly "Alleluia" and also to ask you to do me a little service.

Bringing with you the enclosed letter (a copy of a letter from the American consul in Johannesburg) could you go to the American Embassy, near the Crillon, one of these days, give the letter to whoever handles this sort of thing, and explain to him that I cannot present myself before June 10 to complete the formalities for my visa as a "permanent visitor" (in the capacity of the representative of religion!)? My dossier containing the approbation of the Jo-burg consul must have arrived in Paris by now, and I would appreciate it if you would explain for me that I will present myself at the Embassy when I arrive there.—When you read the letter, you will understand. Thank you.

Otherwise, there is nothing new. I continue the retyping of my manuscript on Man. Much too short. Perhaps too dense. In any case, I've put in it much more than I meant to. Just noticed in the April issue of *Etudes* that the confusion over the idea of the priesthood continues. . . . But it's neither the Theologians nor moralists who will resolve the problem, linked as it is to a rethinking of the relationship between (or better still, to the very notion of) Spirit-Matter. Such a rethinking demands *the integral admission of a generalized evolution.* I had this impression when I read with great sympathy something dear Valensin has written. But what use is it to connect Ethics, Aesthetics, and Metaphysics, if one does not lift the envelope of fog from Historic Reality (as much as possible) through Energetics? And then, in reality, what is "beauty" (and above all "Absolute Beauty"!) if it is not reattached to a cosmic process of Union?—Am I the dreamer?—Or can it be that 95% of the world still have their eyes closed? . . .

Faithfully,
TEILHARD

(I'm waiting to see the Bardacs when they pass through. The San Francisco branch of his bank has been closed! . . .)

New York, May 3, 1954

Dear Friend,

. . . Nothing much is new except for the visit of some interesting Frenchmen (birds of spring for Easter!) notably Jaques Rueff (the socialist-financier whom Russo knows) who has decided upon the project of an "informal" conference between a handful of scholars (physicists, biologists, but *not* anthropologists) in order to see how to attack a serious study of the "Human Phenomenon." It's planned for the end of June, if possible.

I finished my paper on "The Singularities of the Human Species." (Three copies.) But what will I do with it? If I could find a technical review that might be interested (for example, the *Archives de l'Institut de Paléontologie Humaine*) I think that I could publish it without asking anyone for permission, as I did with my lectures at the Sorbonne in 1951. But will the *Archives* buy it—even with a subsidy from Fejos?—I'll really have to see about it with Piveteau. Incidentally, Piveteau is going to present himself for the Academy at the end of May to replace de Margerie. I think he will be elected hands down. But Arambourg is trying for the same appointment. If I found myself in Paris for the elections I would be embarrassed. Arambourg is one of our closest collaborators at the Wenner-Gren on the famous "Project Africa."

There is a good joke going around about de Breuvery at the United Nations: "The best way to keep an eye on him is to only let him work three hours a day." By the way, did you know that the connection between the priest-workers and the priest-technicians (in every area) was made immediately in the minds of "Gentiles"?

Warmest regards always,
TEILHARD

New York, May 13, 1954

Dear Friend,

... Again there is nothing new to tell you. Central Park is green, and I can see the first signs of spring. Spring in such a troubled world!—There seems absolutely no way of resolving the conflict in the Far East. The truth is that, perverted, and concealed under the frightfully ambiguous term "communism," a new "spirit" (what I call "the spirit of the *En Avant*") is spreading irresistibly throughout the world. And Rome, as much as Washington, will be touched by it. I have spent my life in trying to define this new "spirit" and in trying to give it a name. And despite so many disturbing developments, I cannot keep myself from triumphing secretly when I see it emerge. The only, and the great, interest (for it, as for us) is that we reach the point of Christifying it in time. . . .

Most affectionately always,
TEILHARD

Teilhard arrived in France in the beginning of June, just as he had planned, and he took up residence at Etudes once more. He went back to his old desk, and to the parlor where a flood of visitors testified to the continuing influence his thought had in his own country. He went to various meetings, and visits with friends filled the remaining waking hours. At one point, after considerable hesitation, he agreed to give a public conference on prehistoric man. The meeting took place in the Salle des Sociétés Savantes on the Rue Danton. Nervous, tired and worried, Teilhard was not himself; and when he finished, apparently desperate to avoid confronting any of his listeners, he hurried off.

Two days later, he and I took an auto trip together. We went to Auvergne and to Perigord, passing, as a first step, through Lyon where the hill of Fourvière had long been the site of a famous Jesuit house of theological studies. When Teilhard arrived, the young scholastics mobbed him. They plied him with questions and requests for private meetings. Since he loved to communicate to others the vision of reality he so long cherished, and since the reactions which such conversations always evoked served to feed his thought and clarify his views, the warmth and intellectual curiosity of these young students was an enormous comfort to him. He had been deprived of such salutary contacts for much too long.

The next day, in a state of real euphoria he left Lyon. We drove across to Clermont-Ferrand and the little town of Orcines near Sarcenat, one of the great old houses in which Teilhard had grown up. One of his sisters-in-law was waiting for him. Spring sunlight gilded the old chateau, once so full of life, but gloomy now after having been the scene of so many sorrows and disappointments. While we rested, Teilhard doubtless thought of years gone by. Sitting on the terrace in that lovely afternoon in June, he seemed borne away by memory.

Suddenly, though, he rose, and without a word, entered the house. He looked into the drawing room, and then into the dining room dominated by the great round table where he had shared so many family meals. Where happy children's voices once had rung, a deep, cold silence greeted him. It had been here where his family and their servants used to meet after dinner for common prayer. For a while my friend stood still and looked about him. His glance grazed the places against the wall where his brothers and sisters used to kneel and the table itself over which his Mother and Father had reverently bent. In those moments of pious family intimacy, no one had dreamt of what a remarkable feast of thought one of these children was going to set to feed the minds of future generations.

On the second floor, Teilhard stopped before a lady's room and stared inside. It was his mother's bedroom. A pastel portrait of him, done when he was three, hung on the wall. Standing beside him, I was struck by the depth of the dark glance and strange energy that radiated from this conventional picture of a child with curly hair and lacy dress. It was in this room that Teilhard spoke the only phrase he uttered on that afternoon. "This," he murmured almost to himself, "is the room where I was born."

We stayed that night at a nearby inn. The next morning we visited the caves of Lascaux, and then spent several days near Montignac in the heart of a countryside full of monuments to French prehistory. Before returning to Paris, we stopped at Nohant to visit George Sand's house at La Châtre. The building had been kept much as the novelist had left it. In the dining room the table was set with placecards bearing the names of expected guests: Flaubert, Victor Hugo, Balzac. In the park nearby, Madame Sand is buried. While we stopped there, I remembered a story I'd been told about the Abbé Mugnier* who

---

*L'Abbé Arthur Mugnier (1854–1940). French priest, who frequented the salons of his day where he exercised a kind of chaplaincy to the literati. Huysmans was one of his converts. M.L.

was surprised once in tears as he prayed beside the novelist's grave. This strange admiration of the priest for the writer had been confirmed to me by a friend,** *who as a young girl had known the Abbé. One day, after she had read him a text describing "d'arbes, des fleurs, d'une mare aux fées," she said to him, "This pretty scene should please you, M. l'Abbé." He shook his head. "I prefer," he said, " 'la Mare au Diable.' "****

After our return to Paris, life became normal again. All through July, however, my friend seemed extremely uneasy. Even though he told me nothing, I felt he would be leaving very soon.

Finally he told me he had decided to go back to America, stopping en route in England to see Kenneth Oakley and other paleontologists at the British Natural History Museum.

He made the stop, and after he reached America, he wrote me in an attempt to explain his haste in leaving. It had all been too much for him, he said—too many meetings, too many rapid attachments and detachments. Although his trip to France had given him some happiness, clearly it did not turn out the way he hoped.

And too, he had been worried about the still unsettled question of his visa. Without a permanent one, how long would he be permitted to stay in New York? Oddly enough, no one else seemed much distressed about the problem. There was no difficulty at the debarkation, and his friends the Strauses met him at the dock, helped him with his bags, and drove him to their country house at Purchase.

By August 24, he was back in New York City. To his great satisfaction, he found that Father de Breuvery was there, too, just back from Geneva with a definitive appointment to the United Nations. Those "little friends," who would have preferred to be rid of him, and proposed he take an "important" post in far-off Bangkok, had lost out. De Breuvery had sensed

---

**Oral communication to the writer by Madam Jacqueline de la Bégassière de Contades. P.L.

****La Mare au Diable*. 1864 novel by George Sand.

LETTERS FROM MY FRIEND TEILHARD

the trap and refused the transfer, thus strengthening his posi-tion at the heart of United Nations activity in New York.

Purchase, N.Y., August 26, 1954

Dear Friend,

Forgive my long silence. I'm still a little bewildered by those agitated weeks in Paris—by that multiplicity of too-rapid contacts, by a hectic rhythm of attachments and detachments.— However, on the whole I've been satisfied (enlightened and strengthened) by this contact with France. And did I tell you that the two most luminous points of the visit were Lyon and Lascaux? But you know that without my having to tell you.

The return trip was without incident. Except for one day, a calm sea, a full ship (no one interesting abroad), likeable person-nel, a warm reunion with the barmen and the waiters. Marvel-ous food.—The Strauses were waiting for us with a car at the dock. We arrived at about five in the evening and dined at eight in the lovely countryside at Purchase. The London stopover had been agreeable and useful. But I only saw Oakley. Desmond Clarke (from Livingstone) was expected, but we hadn't time to wait for him.—The day before yesterday I had a very pleasant time in New York. I dined with Fejos and de Breuvery. The lat-ter has absolutely settled in N.Y. and refused to accept the high position in Bangkok because he considers his action more im-portant at the New York headquarters. (You will imagine how much his "little friends" here bless him for it!) He seems to be establishing himself more and more in the good graces of Ham-marskjold. He returned from Geneva to New York (by plane) the same day as I arrived (August 16), having seen scarcely any-one in Paris.

Despite the lesson of 1952, the Foundation has embarked on a new symposium (June 1955). Subject: the modification of the earth under human influence. In my opinion, the blocks to its success are the same as they were two years ago.—There are too many participants (more than 50), a confused program, far too many "humanists" and literary people. All the same I'm going to draw the best I can from the situation. While waiting I will make a kind of retreat here—the only kind of retreat which is now materially and physically possible for me. I hope by it to take hold of myself again, and thereby recover the "Ever Greater Christ," and through Him, God as well.

In sum, I think I made the right decision in returning so abruptly to America. We'll be back in New York around September 6 (Labor Day).

Yours as ever,
TEILHARD

Best of everything to Lejay and St. Seine. How are they getting along?

P.S.

Among my tearsheets at *Etudes*, if you can put your hand on them, you'd find: 1.) C.R., AC.SC. 1953 (on the Two Possible Centres of the Human Origins); 2.) l'*Anthropologie* 1954 (Research on Human Origins in Africa). Could you send me a half dozen of them?—I forgot them.—The tearsheets from *l'Anthropologie* should be on the top of one of the two cardboard boxes I left in Rouquette's* room.

That September, at the Wenner-Gren, plans were afoot to organize a symposium for June 1955 on how human influence had changed the earth. Teilhard was asked to collaborate on it, but the subject seemed too vague to him. For the moment he went back to Purchase where he took refuge in silence, making a retreat in which he tried to find himself again.

The next month, he took part in a symposium on the Unity of Human Knowledge at a country house in upper New York

*Robert Rouquette, a Jesuit friend and editor of *Etudes*.

State. The meeting had been organized by Columbia University to celebrate its bicentennial. It was comprised of illustrious men: Julian Huxley, Niels Bohr, Charles Malik and the Christian philosopher Etienne Gilson. The question most discussed was whether or not man "moves" biologically. Opinion was completely split. Teilhard responded positively; Gilson responded negatively.

1955

Bust of Teilhard by Malvina Hoffman

Although I had seen my friend briefly earlier that fall when I passed through New York on my way to a scientific appointment in Chicago, it was not until December 23 that I had the chance to talk to him at length. He and de Breuvery had been staying at the Hotel Fourteen, near the Foundation, while they waited to go back to their rooms at the Jesuit residence on Park Avenue, when the renovations were completed. We spent two days together. I found Teilhard tired; he seemed dispirited, without apparent joy, with nothing of that sunny optimism which had always characterized him. He was quiet and seemed absorbed in meditation.

We took our midday meal in a tiny restaurant quite near the Wenner-Gren Foundation. Without his even bothering to order, a waiter who knew his habits brought him a light sandwich and a cup of coffee, before turning back to me. (Teilhard always took his more substantial meal in the evening at the house of a friend.) While we were returning from the coffee shop to the Foundation, he suddenly stopped. And there in the middle of all the street noises, he spoke the words which are still precious to me because I regard them as the final testament of a great soul: "I can tell you," he said, almost in surprise at the sound of his own voice, "that now I am constantly living in the presence of God!"

LETTERS FROM MY FRIEND TEILHARD

How many sorrows, how much conflict, how many battles it had cost him to reach this point! But neither I nor any of his friends then guessed how very short a way he had to go before that Inhabited Darkness, in which now, at last, he could say he always lived, would shatter into Light.

In 1955, I received only two letters from my friend, Teilhard, one dated January 22, and the other dated April 4, a few days before his death.

In neither of them is there a premonition of his approaching end. His days followed their familiar pattern, made up sometimes of unexpected encounters, as were those with the old friends from China who stopped to see him as they passed through America.

At this time in his life, administrative questions troubled him. He did not really feel secure in New York. Nevertheless, he had to arrange for an extension of his tourist visa for six more months. These small vexations annoyed and paralyzed him. He dared not consider another voyage outside America for fear of not being able to go back. This was one reason he gave for refusing Piveteau's invitation to go to a symposium in Paris in April. But equally important in that decision was a fear of reliving the harassing and complex days of summer 1954. Out of friendship for Piveteau he wrote a few pages on a general problem on which he had already been questioned, that of orthogenesis conceived of as the expression of "the drift of Complexity-Consciousness." He would have preferred that the symposium concentrate on the study of physical, chemical, biological means of "Ultra-Hominization" and, by putting the emphasis on "energetics," leave the study of the past in order to examine the future of man. In other words, he felt an effort must be made to pursue the work of evolution to the level of human socialization. Men of science who made it a point to interest themselves only in phenomena and to religiously avoid anything that smacked of metaphysics were not at home with such an idea. To Teilhard, however, an evolution without an End, without a Point of Arrival, is a drifting boat which floats toward shipwreck.

Death comes like a thief in the night, and Teilhard's, too, had come unexpectedly. His last letter to me, on April 14, had the same tone as those that went before.

Yet he only had a few more days to live. He was already engaged in that invisible current, that dark vortex, where everything becomes ambiguous. It almost seems as if, in order to undergo so luminous a resurrection as he would have, a crucifixion was inevitable. Teilhard suffered the intransigence of Rome right to the end. Even though his visa worries and his unhealed wounds from his last visit to France had delivered him from wanting to return to Europe again, Rome itself, having heard that a symposium was going to be held in Paris in April, wrote to forbid Teilhard's participation.

Another sanction which touched him even more deeply, because it was even more inexplicable, was Rome's prohibition of the translation into German at the hands of some admiring friends at Louvain, of some of his already published works. Such machinations would have discouraged the strongest of us. But Teilhard was made of another mettle. As though he were trying to use the time to catch his breath, he spent those empty days writing two essays which he sent to his Provincial, Andre Ravier, one of the few people who had always understood and defended him. Teilhard had intuitively chosen love and union (affective "energy") as the means which direct the movement of Evolution toward the person of Christ.* His "Christique," the first of the two essays, is a moving testimony of this faith. Having lived the love of God and faith in the world, he had seen its effects in his own person, and was convinced that "the chain" of those who saw reality in the same way would grow.

The second essay he wrote during this time is more practical. It is an invitation to superiors to give a special theological-mystical formation to priests who worked in science or in the factory, an intellectual testament sent to those in power in his

---

*In 1932, he had written to Auguste Valensin: "The one goal of my life . . . will be to work with complete singlemindedness at breaking the circle in which, through a bitter irony, the 'children of the light' have enclosed Spirit . . . . We are dying today from the fact of not having anyone who knows how to lay down his life for the Truth."

LETTERS FROM MY FRIEND TEILHARD

Order. Though persuaded that such a gesture was necessary, Teilhard had no illusions about what the result would be.

"In Rome," he wrote, "this last appeal evidently remains a dead letter."

New York, January 22, 1955

Dear Friend,

By way of Helen Burton (aged but just as sweet, and as eccentrically dressed as ever and whom I ran into unexpectedly at Malvina's) I learned that Vetch is set up again in Hong Kong, "matured, softened, almost spiritualized" by his prison experience. And I'm going to write him.—I still wonder what he knows of the fate of our publications. Does he imagine that the Geobiological Institute will survive in another incarnation on Formosa?—A Chinese paleontologist whom I barely remember (Ko is his name) has just arrived (from Formosa?) at the American Museum. But I haven't seen him yet.—Incidentally, I had a confirmation that Wong had just "gone over to the other side." Can it really be through conviction, or just duty?

Again, there's nothing new in my life.—I'm still a little tangled in my visa troubles. Yesterday, at last, I got a six-month extension of it. In July I'll have another X-ray, and then we'll see about a permanent visa. Meanwhile, I don't want to risk leaving the USA for fear of not being allowed back in. And for this reason, I shall regretfully decline Piveteau's kind invitation to join his symposium at the Sorbonne. (Its subject: "The Present Problems of Paleontology.") The voyage would be paid for. So it's a shame in a sense to miss the opportunity. But after all, it's perhaps better not to repeat the "hectic" experience of a month in Paris.—Finally, in all honesty, I'm not particularly excited by anyone's new impressions of the origins of the Tetrapods, or by discussion of the exact position of the Australopithecines. In other words, right now I'm waiting for the sciences of the Past to rebound on themselves. But now is this to happen?—It seems to me that at the present moment there *are* no vital problems in paleontology. (Everything is more or less resolved, at least in the first approximation, which is the same as saying that the Piveteau symposium does not seem to me properly focused.)—As a sign of sympathy and good will, however, I have written down a few pages to be read *apropos* of orthogenesis, taken in the general and rigorously experimental-phenomenal sense of "the drift of lower Complexity-Consciousness."—To tell the truth, the paper that I would really like to have sent him would be titled: "Are there still any important problems left in Paleontology?" But this would hardly be politic; and psychologically speaking, it could be quite destructive.

The irreplaceable service which paleontology can render is to show us what I call the "drive of Complexity-Consciousness" (Syntropy or Ectropy, as it is now being called by many people). But as far as discovery is concerned, the only really interesting thing left for paleontology to do is to find:

1.) the physical, chemical, biological and social *means* of ultra-hominization—of prolongation of the movement of arrangement; 2.) the *incentive* for continuing to "evolve," to self-evolve.

It is this second "Energetic" point which has fascinated me above all else for a long time. The reality of Evolution (in other words, a "Cosmogenesis" which is a "Noogenesis") is no longer in doubt among people who count. The real problem now is to find a fuel, an *excitant,* and finally a "God" for this Evolution, now that it has become reflective.

There's little news from France.—De Breuvery is fine. Just as he wished, he has gotten a place on the Atomic Energy Commission. But he feels the opposition forming quietly around him. Will his contract be renewed in the spring? Or will they give him a "promotion" out of the country? I think that basically his chances are good, and highly placed friends protect him. He will stay.

Affectionately,
TEILHARD

LETTERS FROM MY FRIEND TEILHARD

New York, April 4, 1955

My dear Friend,

Nothing particularly new in my life now. I spent the winter writing and correcting a few papers, and also handling red tape connected with my passport and visa. Through Washington, I've set in motion a request to obtain a permanent visa—counting on the stabilization of my lung problems which seemed controlled when checked in January, and upon the (clerical) good will of the Immigration Service.—If all goes well and I receive my visa, I hope to go to California (Berkeley) in September, via Panama, if I have my visa.

Would you believe that Rome:

1.) will not give me permission to go to Paris for the paleontological symposium at the Sorbonne in April 1955 to which I was invited by the C.N.R.S.?* Since I don't have a reentry visa I wouldn't have asked to anyway. But to be on the safe side, Ravier had warned me not to, and 2.) put a stop to the proposal made by the House of Benziger (Eiseideln) to publish a German translation of my published articles—an affair which was conducted unbeknownst to me by some S.J. friends from Louvain. "There is no point in spreading these ideas any further," the Fr. General wrote to Ravier ... —It's curious ("anxious" as I am, and remain, on so many points) that I feel absolutely untroubled; on the contrary, I am encouraged or at least excited by these obstacles. Resistance of this kind strengthens me, because I am so very sure that I am saying what is really in the mind and heart of everyone.—Six days ago, I sent to Masson a clean copy of my memoir on "The Singularities of the Human Species" *(Annales de Paléontologie)*, and the W.G. Foundation is publishing my pages on the "Noosphere" as one of the preliminary memoirs to its June symposium at Princeton. I also wrote an essay (a "clandestine") on the "Christique" and a report to Ravier called

*Centre National de la Recherche Scientifique (France's National Center for Scientific Research).

214

"Research, Work and Adoration" about the necessity of a special theological-mystical formation of laboratory priests, researcher-priests and worker-priests.—For Rome this last appeal evidently will remain a dead letter. But I'm sure that eventually the idea will make its way.—By the way, have you ever realized to what a point the "Exercises" (with the divisions: Foundation, Sin, Reign, the Two Standards—everything except the Ad Amorem) are magnificently transposable in terms of a Universe in genesis, where, from this time forward beside (at the base of) "the Supernatural" we must make a place for the Ultra-Human?

De Breuvery fights on, and makes his mark—the last achievement being his important nomination as secretary to the conference on Atomic Energy in August in Geneva. Right now he's being considered for his permanent contract with the United Nations. There are people who want his skin. But it seems he'll overcome without too much difficulty. His health is good, but he's overworked, and he cannot budge until summer . . . .

Good luck . . . .

And most affectionately yours in Christ,
TEILHARD

Two days after this letter arrived, Father de Breuvery telephoned from New York to Chicago where I was working. It was April 10, 1955, Easter Day. In that end of the afternoon in spring (it was scarcely six o'clock) twilight fell over the exuberant life of the city. Gaiety was in the air. Nothing had prepared me to hear the bitter news he brought.

Without any warning of so sudden an end, Pere Teilhard had just been struck down by death . . . in the space of a few minutes. After having celebrated Easter in peace and joy, he had come to the final passage.

I did not see him until Easter Monday. His body was laid in the private chapel of the Jesuit Fathers of St. Ignatius High School. He was dressed in violet vestments, his hands crossed on a rosary and crucifix, and his face a little sunken, he lay in the silence of death. It was, therefore, finished. If I had lost an in-

comparable friend, the world and the Church had lost an uncommon mind which, through so many troubles and misunderstandings, had tried to extend to humanity a message of hope.

I could not lift my eyes to him . . . . I stayed near him and reread his last letter: "I have written a report (Research, Work and Adoration) on the necessity of the special theologico-mystico formation for laboratory–priests, priest–researchers and priest-workers." This then indeed, was the heart of his thought: to rise to the Divine without turning away from the Earth. As I knelt before the coffin, which in a few hours would be closed forever, things that we had so often talked about returned to my mind. I remembered phrases from The Phenomenon of Man. They seemed so full of meaning in this strange exchange.

"When Man individualizes himself, he falls back into Matter; when Man advances with everything else in the direction of the Other, he becomes Person . . . ."

"Human particles cannot come together except under the influence of a colossal force: Love . . . What we need is a universal Love . . . ."

"The World finds its stability in climbing toward a divine Foyer of Spirit, which pulls it forward . . . ."

Everything that he preached, Teilhard had intensely lived. With all the strength of his soul he had believed in the Christ of St. Paul and the Christ of St. John. He had fought for the destiny of collective Humanity moving toward Christ, Master and King of creation. "The great human machine only advances," he has written, "by producing a superabundance of Spirit. If it only brings forth Matter, it will work against itself . . . . The day will come when Man will recognize that, for him science is not an accessory occupation, but the essential form of action . . . . The day will come when Man will realize that it is in order that he might know and be (rather than have) that Life has been given to him . . . . It is not toward endless progress that the world is moving . . . but toward an ecstasy outside the Universe . . . ."

What strength these affirmations assumed before that open coffin! The man who had said them was gone, and I would not see him again in my lifetime.

But his example lives on. As does his timeless message.